Patricia Hewitt is Deputy Director of the Institute for Public Policy Research, and was previously Policy Co-ordinator and Press Secretary to the Rt. Hon. Neil Kinnock MP. She is a well-known journalist and campaigner on women's rights, and was for ten years General Secretary of Liberty. Patricia has a three-year-old daughter and a two-year-old son.

Wendy Rose-Neil is a counsellor, psychotherapist, journalist and broadcaster and is currently family columnist for *Woman's Realm* magazine. She was editor of *Parents* magazine for several years. She lives and works in London and Surrey and has two grown-up daughters.

This book is dedicated, with our love, to our partners Bill Birtles and Frank Kevlin, our children and all our sisters and brothers.

Your Second Baby

Patricia Hewitt and Wendy Rose-Neil

UNWIN
HYMAN

First published in Great Britain by Unwin ® Paperbacks, an imprint of Unwin Hyman Limited in 1990

© Patricia Hewitt and Wendy Rose-Neil, 1990

All rights reserved. No part of this publication may be produced, stored in a retrieval system, or transmitted in any form or by any means, electronic, mechanical, photocopying, recording or otherwise, without the prior permission of Unwin Hyman Limited.

Unwin Hyman Limited
15–17 Broadwick Street
London W1V 1FP

Allen & Unwin Australia Pty Ltd
8 Napier Street, North Sydney, NSW 2060, Australia

Allen & Unwin New Zealand Pty Ltd with the Port Nicholson Press, Compusales Building, 75 Ghuznee Street, Wellington, New Zealand

British Library Cataloguing in Publication Data
Hewitt, Patricia
　Your second baby.
　1. Babies. Home care
　I. Title　II. Rose-Neil, Wendy
　649.122

ISBN 0-04-440608-8

Illustrations by Ros Asquith

Typeset in 10/11 point Ehrhardt by Cambridge Photosetting Services
Printed in Finland by Werner Söderström Oy

Contents

Acknowledgements

Introduction   1

1   Planning your second baby   5
2   Pregnancy, preparation and labour   19
3   The first year   37
4   Growing up   61
5   Partners and fathers   87
6   Life with two – the practicalities   100

Appendix I – *Your rights at work*   114

Appendix II – *Useful organisations*   119

Index   126

Acknowledgements

We have been helped by many people in writing this book. First, we want to thank all the parents who generously gave us their time and shared their experiences with us. We have quoted them extensively, but for obvious reasons we have changed their names and the names of their children. We hope they will enjoy reading this book as much as we enjoyed talking to them.

Second, our thanks go to several people who have contributed information, advice and practical help: Adrienne Burgess; Dilys Daws of the Tavistock Institute of Human Relations, who is also chair of the Child Psychotherapy Trust; Jane Franklin; Deidre Jameson of University College Hospital; Dr Mary Lucas of the Department of Genetics, University College Hospital; Sister Adrienne McMeeking of University College Hospital; Ann McDermid. Third, we are particularly grateful to our editors at Unwin Hyman, Bill Neill-Hall and Clare Ford, who encouraged us and offered constant suggestions for improvement.

Above all, we want to thank our partners, Frank Kevlin and Bill Birtles, for their patient interest and support, and our children – Wendy's for inspiration and encouragement, Patricia's for loving distraction!

Patricia Hewitt
Wendy Rose-Neil

The authors and publishers would like to thank Penguin for permission to quote from *Freedom and Choice in Childbirth*, 1988, by Sheila Kitzinger.

Introduction

'Another baby book?' people asked when we said we were writing this one. 'Why?'

The answer is simple. There are plenty of books on pregnancy, childbirth and children. But there is almost nothing which deals with the special problems and pleasures of having your second, third or fourth baby and bringing up your children to be friends, not rivals.

But pregnancy the second time round isn't the same as the first. And a second or subsequent labour is often very different from the first, with its own, often unexpected difficulties. There is plenty of advice to parents on how to bond with their babies – but this doesn't deal with the challenge of bonding with a baby when you have a jealous toddler at your knees!

Every new baby creates a new family. When you have your first baby, you and your partner settle down to a three-way relationship. A second baby changes everything. Now, you have to worry about the relationship *between* your children, as well as between children and parents. For that reason, too, each child grows up in a different family: the second child, for instance, never has the experience of being an only child, while the pain of jealousy is probably never as great as it can be for the first. Each new child affects the relationships in the rest of the family and, by bringing out different qualities in the parents, changes them too.

Anyone who grew up with brothers and sisters knows how intense their friendships and rivalries can be. The love – and, sometimes, the hatred – between siblings can be one of the most powerful influences in our childhood and our adult lives. It is hardly surprising that so many parents feel helpless when faced with siblings who seem to fight all the time. Many parents believe that they must treat their children 'equally' and feel guilty when they find it impossible to do so.

Until recently, three, four or more children was the norm. Growing up in extended family networks made it easier for parents to cope with the practical and emotional needs of their own growing families. That has changed too. Amongst women born in the 1930s – who are in their 50s today – one-fifth had four children or more. But less than one in ten of the women born in the 1950s will do the same. Two children is now the most common family size.

We have found, in extensive discussions with parents having their second babies, that too many are having to re-invent the wheel. Just look at the simple example of getting your children around. Every guide for new mothers gives extensive advice about carrycots, buggies and prams. But almost nothing is said about the far more complicated question of transporting two.

We hope this book will fill some of these gaps. We have interviewed a number of families about the practical, emotional and financial challenges they face, and how they've dealt with them. We have also drawn on the most up-to-date information about child development and family psychology in order to provide practical suggestions for dealing with the common problems of bringing up brothers and sisters. We do not believe there are 'right' and 'wrong' answers: but we firmly believe that there are answers that will work for you. So throughout this book, the emphasis is on tips and strategies that you can use as parents and partners.

The book is arranged in the following way: Chapter 1 is for parents who haven't yet decided whether or when they want another baby. We look at the pressures on parents of one child to have another and discuss the advantages and disadvantages of having an only child. We also talk about the difficulties faced by parents who only want a boy (or, more rarely, a girl). We deal with the question of how to decide what the best age gap between your children will be – as well as how to avoid an accidental pregnancy! We also look at the unexpected problems faced by some parents who find, after their first child is born, that they can't conceive a second.

Chapter 2 looks at pregnancy and childbirth the second time round. This is the time to start preparing your child for the arrival of a sibling; it's also the time for your partner to develop a close relationship with your older child, if he doesn't have that already. We explain in detail the different tests which you may be offered with this baby which you didn't have last time, and we discuss just why a second labour can be very different from the first – and how you can prepare for it most effectively.

Chapter 3 deals with the early days and months after your new baby is born. We suggest ways in which, right from the beginning, you can help your older child get on well with the baby, and how to deal with the anger, the sadness and the jealousy that first children often feel.

Chapter 4 looks at the years of growing up. We deal with the problem of treating your children 'equally' and the dangers of stereotyping them. We suggest ways of helping your children learn to share and to cooperate – as well as ways of coping on those days when they seem to do nothing but fight!

Chapter 5 is for men – as fathers and as partners. We believe that men can be just as good at caring for their children as women, but we also know that the pressures of earning a living make it difficult for men to combine a job with real involvement in their family. We look at paternity leave, and how to argue for paid time off. We suggest ways of building a closer relationship with your children as well as supporting your partner. And we also look at how you can build an even closer relationship with your partner. We hope women will also find it useful.

Chapter 6 looks at the practicalities – time, space, money, child care and transport. One of the biggest problems for growing families is organising time and deciding on priorities. We explain how to avoid the 'Supermum' trap and juggle your different lives in ways that will suit you all. And we give detailed advice on several problems, including the vexed question of transporting two or more children in buggies, cars and public transport.

Finally, we've added two appendices. The first deals with your rights to maternity leave the second time round. The second lists names and addresses of organisations who can offer further help and information.

We are both mothers of two. But we have contributed very different kinds of experience to writing *Your Second Baby*. Wendy, with two daughters now in their twenties, has been able to look back on two decades of parenthood. Patricia, who has a three-year-old daughter and a son of two, is still grappling with the immediate problems of helping two small children become friends, not rivals. Both of us are first children (Wendy with four brothers and sisters, Patricia with three), who know at first hand just how much siblings matter.

Wendy has also been able to draw on eighteen years' professional work as a psychotherapist and counsellor, helping individuals, couples and families at difficult times in their lives. As a former editor of *Parents* magazine, and now family columnist for *Woman's Realm*, she knows just what concerns parents most. Until recently, she was active in The Parent Network, a new national charity of parents' self-help groups.

Patricia is a campaigner for women's rights who was general secretary of Liberty (the National Council for Civil Liberties) for nearly ten years. As policy co-ordinator for the Leader of the Opposition, the Rt. Hon. Neil Kinnock MP, and now as Deputy Director of the Institute for Public Policy Research, she has a particular interest in policies that affect working families. She is also the author of several guides to people's rights, and has answered readers' letters on legal and welfare problems for *Company* magazine and the *Daily Star* newspaper.

Between us, we hope we have identified – and answered – most, if not all, of the questions which parents planning a second child or bringing up two or more children usually face. We would welcome *your* comments and suggestions for material which could be included in future editions of *Your Second Baby*.

Inevitably, a lot of this book is about problems. But it is also about the pleasure of having more than one child, and the unique richness which two or more children bring to your life. One of the mothers we spoke to while we were writing this book summed up how many parents feel, when she told us:

> Of course there are times when we are all at screaming point, me included. But then there are the times which really matter, when I watch Sally teaching Richard the song she's just learnt at nursery, or when they both crawl into our bed and lie down hugging each other. That's when never having enough time or money becomes unimportant. Having the two of them has enriched our lives in ways we never dreamt of and I know that with a little bit of luck, even after we are gone, they will be friends for life.

A Note About Style
Rather than refer to your first child throughout the book as either 'he' or 'she', we have compromised by using 'he' and 'she' in alternate chapters.

1 Planning your second baby

Some people know exactly how many children they want even before they have their first baby. If you both come from a large, happy family yourself, you may find the idea of only having one or two children unthinkable. But some parents of only children know from the beginning that they don't want more than one child.

For other people, the decision is more difficult. Will having a second baby make our first child miserable? If we don't have another, will our first child suffer from being an 'only'? Will we be able to cope with another baby? Can we afford another child? If I take another maternity leave, will I be able to get back to work again later? In this chapter, we look at these and other questions which parents have talked to us about.

Having another baby makes a big difference to your lives. One of the fathers we spoke to described it like this: 'With one baby, we were a couple who happened to have a baby. Now we've got two children, we suddenly feel like a real family.'

Once you've had your first child, the pressures on you to have a second can be surprisingly strong. Your parents and in-laws may long for several grandchildren. (One mother told us that her only child was presented by her grandmother with a book called *Your New Baby Brother!*) Your partner may long for a baby of the other sex. You may feel that your first child will miss out by being an 'only'.

If you're in two minds about whether or not to become pregnant again, don't try and rush the decision. Giving yourself and your partner time to think about it is going to make things much easier for you and your child – and your next baby, if you do decide to go ahead. Cheryl was very happy with her first baby and enjoyed going back to work after several months' maternity leave. She told us:

> The problem is that Stephen has already decided he wants another. He'd really like us to get pregnant straight away. I feel with a job and a seven-month-old I've got enough on my hands already. We can still do all the things we like doing – we just take the baby with us. But I look at friends with two children whose lives seem much more restricted.

Cheryl persuaded Stephen to wait a year before starting another baby.

If you had a very difficult first labour or suffered from postnatal depression, then you need to give yourself enough time to recover before thinking about a second baby. But even without these special considerations, many mothers feel for quite a long time that another pregnancy and another baby is the last thing they need! Unfortunately it's very easy to get pregnant by accident after you've had a baby; see the section on contraception (page 11) for advice on how not to get caught out.

DO YOU WANT AN ONLY CHILD?

Some parents who aren't sure about wanting a second child feel that they 'ought' to have another for the sake of their first. 'It'll be a playmate for her,' they say, or 'I don't want my first to be an only child.' If you or your partner are still unsure about whether to have a second baby, you may find it very useful to talk about how you feel about having an only child. Lucy and Roger never wanted more than one child, as Lucy explained:

> We adore Timmy and we want to give him everything we can. But we also have very full lives of our own. Roger is a writer who's beginning to be quite successful, and I run my own business. We know that if we have another baby, we'd have less time for Timmy, ourselves and our work. We'd also have less money. It just doesn't seem fair on any of us.

Family finances, not having enough space at home, your own health and that of your child may contribute to your feeling that you don't want another child – at least not yet. Parents of only children, like Lucy and Roger, are usually very happy with the balance they can strike between caring for their child and spending time with each other or on their work. (Some parents find that, although they have one child, they can't get pregnant again; we discuss this situation later, on page 16.)

Other parents talk about the importance of giving their first child at least one sister or brother. Alison is one of three sisters herself.

As a child myself, I thought the word was 'lonely' – I didn't realise until much later that it was 'only' child – because we went to school with a girl who was an only child who seemed such a figure of pathos – even though we were always fighting at home. She used to come round and say 'how wonderful to have people to play with all the time.'

Of course a new baby won't be an instant playmate for your child. But most of the parents we talked to felt that from a very early age, their children were tremendously important to each other. Cathy summed up the mixture of love and rivalry, even hatred, which featured in so many families:

> They always seem to be fighting. I can't bear it – my own two precious babies beating hell out of each other. But then I see Jonathan holding his brother's hand as they go to school together, and he's so proud of Alex, it's wonderful. Or I watch them at home, Alex chasing Jonathan and making him laugh. They are so involved with each other.

It's also important to remember that brothers and sisters will always be part of each other's lives, for good or ill. When we started writing this book we were struck by the number of people who reacted very strongly to any mention of siblings. One man in his fifties, a successful businessman and father of grown-up children himself, told us forcefully: 'I was four when my brother was born. It ruined my life and I've never recovered from it.' His was perhaps an extreme reaction, but it certainly wasn't unique. Your oldest child won't necessarily thank you for giving him a brother or sister.

On the other hand, an only child has to face milestones in his life, like the death of a parent, without a brother or sister. Alison recalls a conversation with a friend whose mother had died recently.

> She's an only child and because of that, there's no one else who sees it from the same point of view. Her friends have been good, but there comes a time when they don't want to listen to her talking about her mother any longer. Only a brother or sister would be suffering the same loss, in the same position as her.

Having another baby can enrich your first child's life, as well as your own. Dilys Daws, a child psychotherapist at the Tavistock Institute in London, describes it in this way: 'Children are born with different personalities. As a parent, your different children pull something different out of you. You actually become a richer person as you have your different children. And I should think your children benefit from having parents who have been stretched emotionally.'

Advantages of an only child

- You and your partner are free to give all your attention to one child, who will benefit from maximum adult stimulation. You will have time to do the other things that you enjoy.
- One child can easily be fitted into your lives – work, travel, social

activities and so on. With two or more children, your lives may be much more restricted.
- Your child never has to suffer sibling rivalry and jealousy. And you never have to cope with children at war with each other.
- If you're a single parent, having another child may create too many financial as well as emotional stresses.

Disadvantages of an only child

- Your child misses out on the closeness which only siblings can offer – not only in childhood, but also in adulthood. He won't have the advantage of learning to share and cooperate with other children at home; he'll have to learn it all elsewhere.
- You won't have the experience of loving another child and learning to respond to his or her different needs.
- An only child may feel out of it at school, since most other children will have one or more siblings. Teachers, books and school projects often assume that children have brothers or sisters.
- Your grown-up only child will have to cope with your growing old on his own. You can't guarantee that you will never become frail or senile: it would be easier for two or more children to share the burden.

MORE THAN TWO?

Family sizes have been falling in most Western countries. In Britain, for instance, 20 per cent of women born in 1935 had four children, compared with only 12 per cent of women born ten years later. Younger women are having even fewer children, and two children is now the most common family size.

Just as a second child means a big change in your lives, so does a third or fourth. Mary is the mother of five boys:

> If you're two parents and two children, you've always got the possibility of each of you looking after one child, if one of them's ill for instance. When you've got three, that's no longer an option – you're into a completely different way of being a family. With three, I think it's always two plus one. There's a very big difference again between three children and more than three.

Alison finds advantages in a larger family:

> In theory, three's a disadvantage. But you can be an outgroup of one in a family of four. There's no guarantee of good relationships whatever number you have. But what's nice about three is that if Tom and Dick have an argument and Dick loses, Lucy will comfort him. There's an extra person available to mediate. Three's good – it takes the intensity out of it a bit.

Mary agrees:

> If you've got two children competing for attention, it is very easy to build up 'You love her more than me.' That doesn't happen with big families. When I give the youngest a lot of time, the others will look on in disgust; they feel wronged, but they can't take it personally! They're all in it together. There are disadvantages to being so many, but that's one of the big advantages – it's not always 'him or me'.

For each couple, it's a question of when you feel complete. For some people, that feeling comes after only one child, or with two children. For others, it only comes with a very large family. Deciding when you feel complete can be more difficult, however, if one of you already has children from a previous marriage.

SECOND FAMILIES

The decision about whether or not to have another child can be particularly difficult in a second relationship, as Jonathan explains:

> I already have two grown-up daughters from my first marriage. One of them got married herself the other day. Margaret and I have a three-year-old daughter. For Margaret, Katie is her only child. For me, she's my third. I'm nearly forty-five, I don't really want another baby, I want some time to myself and I want more time with Margaret. But she feels that she may regret not having another baby before it's too late.

If your partner is supporting his first family financially, then you may feel you simply can't afford another child. It can be very difficult dealing with the resentments and rivalries which can build up between the two families. And if, like Jonathan and Margaret, having another child means quite different things, it may be difficult to come to a decision you both feel happy with. Margaret and Jonathan decided to see a family counsellor to help them talk about the problem. In Appendix II we list possible sources of help.

For Ann, who is a single mother, the decision to have a third child was even more difficult because her new partner is black and both were aware of the problems of bringing up a mixed-race child in a society which discriminates against black people. Her own family weren't much help; when Rebecca was born, Ann's mother's first comment was: 'Just how black is she?'

Ann says that she really thought very hard about whether or not to have a third baby:

> I was worried about how it would affect Elizabeth and Charley. I knew there would be all kinds of extra difficulties in having a black child. I had to work out whether I would really regret not having a third child later, even though I knew it would put a lot of pressures on me in the early years. But the nub of the decision was whether having a third baby would have a bad effect on Elizabeth and Charley. If I'd thought

they were going to suffer emotionally or financially, I wouldn't have done it. In the end I decided on balance they wouldn't lose out – and in fact their lives have been enriched by having this younger sister, and by having a black sister.

A LATE ADDITION TO YOUR FAMILY

Some couples already have teenage or adult children when they decide to have another baby, or become pregnant by accident. There seems to be an unexplained fertility peak in women at about thirty-nine or forty, and some women in their forties find themselves pregnant when they thought they were starting the menopause.

It can be difficult to start all over again with bringing up a baby when you already have a grown-up family. You and your partner may find broken nights and the baby's demands far more tiring, and may not enjoy the prospect of having a teenage son or daughter when you yourselves are retired. On the other hand, 'afterthought' children can bring enormous joy to their parents and their older siblings. With a large age gap, problems of jealousy and sibling rivalry are rare. You and your partner may find you enjoy being parents more this time round just because you're secure about yourselves and what you want from life.

WANTING A BABY OF THE 'RIGHT' SEX

Strange though it may seem, one of the biggest sources of disappointment to many parents is not having a child of the 'right' sex. According to several research studies, almost twice as many parents want their first child to be a boy. In one survey, 90 per cent of parents with a boy were happy with their child's sex, compared with only half of the parents who had a girl. This preference for boys is widespread in many different countries and cultures. The reasons for it are complex and deeply rooted in historical and cultural traditions which entrench men's greater power and status – like passing on the family name and property through the father. With the increasing economic power of women, and equal legal status between the sexes, this preference for sons may gradually weaken. But meanwhile many parents will continue to be disappointed in not having a son.

Some parents decide to have another baby in order to get the sex they prefer. But this isn't a very good reason for enlarging your family. There is, after all, a strong possibility that you'll end up with a baby of the 'wrong' sex. (There are occasional press reports about parents having an abortion when they discover the sex of their foetus. Any abortion performed on such grounds would, of course, be illegal.)

Small children very quickly discover that their parents really wanted a child of the opposite sex. In some extreme cases, parents may simply not realise the extent to which their children are living up to these wishes.

One mother of two boys described how she'd longed for a girl the second time round:

> My older boy – he's a real little boy. Just like his dad. Very tough, he hates to be hugged and kissed. But my younger boy – he's just like a girl, really. He's always wanting to dress up in girls' clothes and he even asks me to paint his fingernails!

Some parents whose first two children are the same sex may have a third or even a fourth child in the hope of concciving the longed-for boy or girl. There is a real danger that the third and fourth children, particularly, will feel painfully rejected by their parents. For example, one third-born we talked to spoke of her experience as an adult going to a counselling group after her divorce:

> We each had to introduce ourselves and say a few things about who we were. When it came to my turn, I said 'I'm Robin, I'm the third of four children and my parents gave me a boy's name because they really wanted a boy.' I didn't even know I was going to say it until the words came out and I burst into tears.

If you do feel your baby is the wrong sex, it's important for your child's sake to try and come to terms with the fact that you have the boy or girl you didn't want. Your child may never reproach you openly for your disappointment, but he or she will certainly carry the resentment at a deeper level inside, which in turn may make future relationships more difficult.

The best reasons for having another baby are just the same as the reasons for having your first: you want to create and love and nurture another human being. If you really feel that you only want a boy, then perhaps you should think again about having another baby.

AVOIDING AN ACCIDENTAL PREGNANCY

As you lie in bed recovering from your first baby's birth, you may be appalled to find your midwife, doctor and nurses all talking to you about contraception! The thought of making love – let alone another pregnancy and labour – may be more than you can bear.

But the obsession with contraception for new mothers is entirely practical. It is often much easier to get pregnant the second time round. If you had difficulty conceiving your first baby, do not assume it will be difficult again the next time round: in fact, you may conceive immediately.

Breastfeeding does not protect you against another pregnancy. One piece of research found that *full* breastfeeding, and the complete absence of periods, does provide a high level of contraceptive protection. At six months, however, if periods return or you have reduced the level of breastfeeding before then, the risk of pregnancy increases. You may start ovulating again, and get pregnant, before you have another period and realise that you're at risk. So you should never rely on breastfeeding to protect you against pregnancy.

Getting pregnant before you are ready may be bad for your health, as well as very distressing. It makes far more sense to talk to hospital staff and to your own doctor or health centre about what kind of contraception will work best for you.

Joanna got pregnant by accident:

> We enjoyed our first baby so much, we decided we would have another – but not until Sally was about two. We wanted to go on enjoying our time with her before having a second. I started using the cap after she was born, although I always found it quite difficult to get inserted properly. But I'd had trouble conceiving before, so I wasn't too bothered, and I didn't use the spermicide jelly either. When Sally was eleven months old, I discovered to my horror I was already three months pregnant. I was unhappy about it for months, and so was my husband. Even after Richard was born, it took us quite some time to settle down and start enjoying both children.

CONTRACEPTIVE METHODS

It is not always easy to find a contraceptive method that will suit you if you are thinking of having another baby. You need to talk to your partner and your doctor or family planning clinic about what is best for you both. Contraceptive supplies from your GP or a family planning clinic are free; the sheath and contraceptive sponge can also be bought without a prescription at a chemist.

Using a *sheath* is effective and, unlike other contraceptives, has no side-effects. You can also use a spermicide to give extra protection. Their failure rate is between 2 and 15 per cent, but properly used they are as effective as other contraceptives. If your partner objects to using a sheath, you need to talk to him about the risks for you of other methods (particularly the pill).

The *contraceptive pill* provides a very high level of protection against pregnancy. There are two kinds: the 'combined pill' (failure rate 1–2 per cent) and the 'mini-pill' (failure rate 1–4 per cent).

The combined pill, although extremely effective, is unsuitable while you are breastfeeding since the hormones which it contains will get into your milk and could affect the baby. Even after you have stopped breastfeeding, it will not be suitable if you are a smoker, have high blood pressure or a history of heart disease in your close family. The combined pill can produce side-effects which include headaches, sore breasts, nausea, weight gain and depression.

The mini-pill (which contains progesterone only, not oestrogen) can be taken while you are still breastfeeding. But it has to be taken at exactly the same time every day in order to be reliable. Some women find that it causes headaches, while others suffer from breakthrough bleeding.

Although an *intrauterine device* (IUD or coil) also has a low failure rate (1–3 per cent), most doctors do not recommend it if you are thinking of having another baby, since in a few cases it can cause pelvic inflammatory disease which could make it difficult or impossible for you to get pregnant again.

The *diaphragm or cap* provides a reasonable level of protection (failure rate 2–15 per cent) and has no side-effects. It needs to be used with a spermicide as well. If you were using a cap before your first pregnancy, it is *essential* to get fitted with a new one since the old one will almost certainly be too small.

Another possibility is the *contraceptive sponge* which can be bought at a chemist or obtained free from family planning clinics (not your GP). The sponge contains spermicide and can be inserted into the vagina up to twenty-four hours before intercourse; it must then be left in place for at least six hours afterwards. It is safe to use during breastfeeding, although it cannot be used during a period. It has a rather high failure rate (9–25 per cent) but would be an alternative to a sheath if you and your partner would prefer to postpone pregnancy yet wouldn't be distressed by an earlier one.

If you are pretty sure that you don't want another baby, but neither of you wants to be sterilised, at least not yet, then you need a contraceptive method which is very reliable. In these circumstances, you might want to use the pill, although the cap or sheath could also be suitable. But if you and your partner do plan another baby, but would prefer a longer age gap, then an accidental pregnancy would be less of a problem and you might well not want to risk the side-effects of using the pill.

IS THERE AN IDEAL GAP BETWEEN BABIES?

Many parents who have decided to have another baby want to know if there's a right time to get pregnant the second time. Is there less jealousy if the babies are close together? Is it easier to cope with the second if you've already got your first child settled in nursery school?

It is widely believed that the age gap does affect the reaction of the first child. Some psychologists suggest that jealousy is likely to be particularly severe when the age difference is between one-and-a-half and three years. Some of the parents we spoke to felt that a very small gap (one to about one-and-a-half) made things easier since the older child had not yet got used to the idea of being an 'only' child.

Some research has been done in Britain and the United States about the effect of different age gaps between brothers and sisters. Some studies from the USA have found that children who are less than two years apart were closer, disliked being separated and often played with each other and with the same friends. In those studies, children four to six years apart seemed much less involved with each other.

The age gap, however, seems to make virtually no difference to the older child's reaction to the baby's birth, at least if the older child is under five. The under-five child is likely to be disturbed by the birth of a second baby, at least for a while – but whether the older child is fifteen months old or nearly five doesn't really matter.

The biggest study in Britain on siblings was carried out by Judy Dunn and Carol Kendrick, who followed forty families in Cambridgeshire who were expecting a second baby. They visited the families before the second baby was born and again three times after the birth, until the second child was fourteen months old. The age gap between the first and second children ranged from eighteen months to forty-three months. They found that younger children tended to become more clingy after the second baby's birth, but that otherwise the age gap made no differences.

The Cambridge study found that other things had a more important effect than the age gap on how well the children got on together in the twelve months or so after the new baby's birth. These include your relationship with your first child; the sex of the two children; how close the father is to his first child (before and after the second baby is born) and your first child's temperament.

For instance, according to this study, a first child who was generally 'negative' before the baby was born – difficult to settle, often crying or cross – was more likely to become very clinging after the arrival of the baby. A more withdrawn first child may show less interest and affection for the baby than a more outgoing child.

Boys and girls in the Cambridge study often reacted differently to the birth of a sibling. Boys were generally more likely to be withdrawn. Where the mother had a very close relationship with a first-born daughter (particularly in a family where the father was out all day, there were no grandparents living nearby, and the mother and daughter were rarely if ever apart), the arrival of a second baby often upset the older daughter considerably.

Not surprisingly, the mother's own reaction to the second baby's birth affected the older child too. Where the mother was very tired or depressed after the birth, the first child was likely to be more withdrawn. In this situation, however, the children often got on better, and there is other evidence to suggest that even very young children turn to each other for support if a parent is ill or unavailable.

So you don't need to worry about choosing the 'ideal' age gap; it doesn't exist! But you and your partner might want to think about what is likely to suit both you and your older child best.

WHAT AGE GAP WILL SUIT THE MOTHER?

First, think about your own health. You will not be back to full physical strength for about twelve months after your first baby. Having two babies within eighteen months or so can be quite a strain physically as well as emotionally. You will be at greater risk of anaemia and, even if you don't suffer from it, you will probably feel more tired the second time round. A longer gap may be better for your own health.

If your first labour was very difficult, or you suffered from postnatal depression, you may need longer to recover. An early second pregnancy could be very distressing for you, while a longer gap would make it easier for you to overcome the fears which your earlier experience may have left you with.

On the other hand, if you are an older mother, it may be desirable to have your second baby sooner rather than later. The risks of having a Down's Syndrome baby increase with age and, for most women, pregnancy itself becomes more tiring the older you are.

If you went back to your job after your first baby's birth, then you need to think about your work situation too. If you want to go back to work again after your second child is born, then you should check whether you will be entitled to another paid maternity leave. (See page 114 for more information.) You may feel that being away from work twice within a few years would jeopardise your chances of promotion. Or you might prefer to have your babies close together, take two lots of maternity leave, and then go back to work knowing that there won't be another break.

You might also want to consider the practicalities of organising life with two. Alison, who has three children with less than four years between the oldest and youngest, says:

> With very young children, remember two is not twice as much work – it's fifteen times as much! The disadvantage of small age gaps is that they all fight. The advantage is the economy of scale – they all want much the same thing at much the same time and it's easier to organise family holidays and outings.

Some parents prefer to get the older child out of nappies and fully potty-trained before embarking on a second baby. Others find it easier to have two babies in nappies and get it all over with as soon as possible. Similarly, having two babies close together means coping with double buggies. Waiting a little longer can be easier. (In Chapter 6, you'll find practical advice on coping with two.)

WHAT WILL SUIT YOUR OLDER CHILD?

You might also consider what age gap would suit your older child best. If, for instance, your first baby was difficult to settle and is still a clinging or nervous child, you may decide to give him more time to become more secure and perhaps to settle into a playgroup and develop his own social life before presenting him with a sibling.

If you have a thoroughly sociable, confident older child, you may well feel that it wouldn't be a good idea to give him too long a taste of being the only child.

You may also have firm ideas about the kind of relationship which you hope your children will have with each other. Obviously, two children who are close in age are more likely to share activities and even friends than children who are several years apart. But that will also be affected by the sex of the second baby – which you can't control. A brother and sister, even when they're close in age, will tend to play with children of their own sex as they grow older.

Thinking through how you and your partner feel and what might work best for you and your first child should help you make the decision which will be right for you. The following checklist summarises the most common advantages and disadvantages which parents mention with regard to the age gap.

Having a small gap between babies

Advantages	*Disadvantages*
May be closer relationship between the children	You may not be fully recovered from the first; risk of anaemia higher
Getting it all over with at once (especially nappies!)	More difficult to cope with two babies at once
If you're an older mum, there may not be much time left; leaving a long gap increases risk of Down's Syndrome	More expensive; you may need two cots and double buggy
If you're planning to stay home while both children are young, having them close together will mean that you can go back to work sooner	Older child less able to help with baby

Having a big gap between babies

Advantages	*Disadvantages*
Older child may be more settled and find it easier to cope	Starting again with nappies and broken nights
You can give your first child all your attention for some years; then concentrate on the second when the older one has started nursery	A large gap may mean the children are less close
Older child can enjoy helping with the baby, and may become a 'teacher' as they grow older	If you're working you'll need different child care arrangements for each child
It's cheaper: second child can use the same cot, buggy and other equipment	

HAVING TROUBLE GETTING PREGNANT AGAIN

Planning your second baby is all very well if you find it easy to conceive. It's useless if you are having trouble getting pregnant.

If you had trouble getting pregnant the first time, then you may be prepared for difficulties the second time round. If you consulted your doctor or were referred to a fertility clinic for help then, you'll know what to do this time.

But if you found it easy to conceive your first baby, it can be a tremendous shock not to get pregnant when you want to again. 'Secondary infertility' – not being able to conceive again after you've already had a child – is more common than you would expect. There are many possible causes, including changes in your hormonal balance or some damage to your fallopian tubes, womb or ovaries from your first childbirth. Fertility also declines with the age of both partners. But often doctors simply cannot find an explanation for secondary infertility, and not knowing the cause can be particularly distressing.

If you are having difficulty conceiving your second baby, then you should ask your GP for help. If you are an older mother, or if you and your partner feel very strongly that you want your children born close together, then it's important to get referred to an infertility clinic or specialist quickly. Even after the referral is made, it may be some months before you get an appointment. Encouragingly, many couples find that they become pregnant while they are waiting to visit the clinic: the reassurance of knowing that help is being offered seems to be enough!

Several tests can be done to try and find out why you and your partner haven't conceived again. Checks are made on your partner's sperm count, and you will probably be asked to keep a record of your morning temperatures to see if you are ovulating normally. You may be asked to make love a few hours before coming for an appointment, so that the presence of sperm in your vagina can be checked. Other tests include laparoscopy, where a small instrument is used to check your womb, ovaries and tubes.

Testing and treatment for infertility can take a very long time and be very intrusive. Many couples say that their love-making loses all its spontaneity because of the need to try and make love within a few days before ovulation, or just before a clinic appointment.

Unfortunately, you may find it more difficult to get help because you already have one child. Because there aren't enough resources for infertility treatment to help all the couples who want it, some clinics are less willing to help older women and give priority to couples who have no children.

If you are in this situation yourself, however, you will know that having one child already does not make the infertility easier to bear. Indeed, watching your child grow up without a sister or brother can make the pain even greater. Not surprisingly, you may find yourself becoming very depressed. If that does happen, it is very important to get help for the depression rather than let this problem spoil your pleasure in your child and your partnership.

Caroline and Michael started trying to become pregnant when their daughter, Jill, was two. After several months, they began getting worried and asked their GP to refer them to a specialist. As Caroline explained:

> The doctors couldn't find anything wrong in the initial tests. We decided we couldn't face going through months and months of treatment, and perhaps not succeeding even then. We were very sad about it, and we went on hoping that we would get pregnant. But I was

determined not to let it spoil my life. I thought about the other things I wanted to do, which would be more difficult if I did have another baby – so I went off and did a degree, which I'd always wanted to do, and went back to work when Jill started school. We still sometimes think it would have been lovely to have another child, but we're so happy with Jill – nothing could spoil that.

2 Pregnancy, preparation and labour

Every pregnancy is different. It's often much easier the second time round, because you know what to expect and you're used to dealing with the doctors and midwives. But you may have had a very difficult pregnancy or labour with your first child, which can affect how you feel this time. And sometimes there are unexpected difficulties too.

The first thing you may find is that other people react to your second pregnancy quite differently from the first. For other people as well as for you, your first pregnancy, your decision to become a mother, is a big milestone. Becoming pregnant again simply doesn't have the same significance for most of the people around you that it will have for you and your partner.

So you may be disappointed to find that even close friends and family aren't as excited as they were before. Your employer may have accepted your first pregnancy and maternity leave without any difficulty, but may give the impression that expecting *two* lots of leave is just self-indulgent! (See page 114 for your legal rights to antenatal and maternity leave.)

If you're having your second baby very soon after your first, or if this is your third or fourth child, you may even receive very hurtful comments. 'Isn't it a bit soon?', 'You're *always* pregnant', 'An accident was it?' or 'How on earth are you going to cope?' are just some of the examples we've heard about.

It helps if you don't count on other people to repeat the delight they expressed the first time round. *You* know how important the baby is to you and, if you're lucky, grandparents as well as good friends will fully share your pleasure.

HOW YOU FEEL DURING PREGNANCY

You may also feel quite different during this pregnancy. For instance, it's quite common for a second pregnancy to show more quickly, since your stomach muscles may not be as firm as they were the first time round and your womb will be stretched from the first birth. If you're having a second baby soon after the first, you may never have managed to get your muscle strength back and it can be very depressing to find that you're having to abandon ordinary clothes much sooner than you want to. It's a good idea to ask your midwife for exercises to help tone up your stomach muscles.

20 YOUR SECOND BABY

With a bit of luck, you will be able to wear many or all of the maternity clothes you had last time. But if you got maternity clothes for the summer, and now have a winter pregnancy, or the other way round, then you may need some additional items. You've probably got less money to spend on yourself this time, particularly if you gave up your job, so it's a good idea to see if you can borrow from friends or buy second-hand. Your antenatal clinic or child's playgroup is often a good source.

If it's a long time since your last pregnancy, you'll find that maternity fashions have changed a good deal. Stretchy lycra leggings and loose tops make a welcome change from maternity pinafores and dungarees! Casual clothes like this are also perfect if you're looking after your child full time. If you need something very smart for a special occasion, you may be able to find a maternity clothes hire agency in your town.

It's also very important to watch how you stand and sit. Tiredness, having to lift an older child, sagging muscles and feeling bad about the way you look can all contribute to drooping shoulders and painful backache. It's worth making a conscious effort to straighten your shoulders, pull in your bottom – and kneel down or bend your knees when you're picking up something (or someone) heavy. You might find it helps to buy some massage oil and use it on your tummy, or get your partner to rub your back.

You may also be even more tired during this pregnancy than during your first. And of course it's much more difficult to make time to rest when you also have a toddler to care for, or if you're combining broken nights with a full-time job, or have to get older children to school and organise their meals and other activities. If you are at home and your child still takes a daytime nap, try to put everything else aside and lie down at the same time yourself.

Nor surprisingly, you can easily become anaemic, especially if your second pregnancy has followed soon after your first. That is another reason why it's very important to attend the antenatal clinic regularly. If you are anaemic, your doctor or midwife may recommend iron tablets. But you should make sure your diet is rich in iron; liver, spinach and other dark green leafy vegetables like watercress, egg yolk, brewer's yeast, nuts, whole grains and pulses (such as lentils) are all good sources.

Anaemic or not, you're going to need all the rest you can possibly get. Ask your partner, if he isn't already doing it, to take your other child or children out for several hours on Saturday or Sunday. *Don't* use the time for housework. If you find it hard to go back to bed when there's a load of dirty washing or washing-up waiting to be done, try to tell yourself that your new-born baby is much more important than the dishes and that the baby needs the sleep just as much as you do. (There is plenty of research to show that the foetus grows most rapidly when the mother is asleep.) If you're on your own, or your partner simply can't or won't help, do try and ask a friend, neighbour or relative to come and help.

If you're at work full time, see if you can arrange to take a short nap or put your feet up during the lunch-break or afternoon. With some jobs – and some bosses – that won't be possible. But if there is a staff restroom, do take advantage of it. You may feel that you have to prove that you can go on working just as hard as you did before, particularly if there is any resentment about the idea of a second maternity leave. But you will work better if you aren't dropping with exhaustion.

If everything is really getting on top of you, *ask for help*. If you're working, take a few days off and go to bed – and if necessary, get your doctor to agree that you need sick leave. If you're a full-time mother and your child isn't going to a playgroup or nursery, ask your midwife or health visitor if there is a local group or childminder who could help.

YOUR MIDWIFE AND DOCTORS

You may also find that the attitude of your doctors and midwives changes with a second pregnancy. Joanna told us:

> The first time I was pregnant, my GP, the midwife and the consultant were all terribly attentive – particularly because I was quite old and had already had one miscarriage. But the second time round they were much more matter-of-fact. With the first, they were worried throughout because I put on very little weight, and by the end they were checking the baby every few days to make sure she was still growing. This time, they didn't seem at all worried even though my weight gain was just as small. But because I'd had very good care the first time, and knew my doctors well, I was quite happy that they weren't fussing!

You may be very lucky and have an easy, trouble-free pregnancy. If you were very sick with the first baby, you may have little or no sickness this time round – although unfortunately, it can also work the other way. If you do find you're suffering from nausea or sickness, it may help to:

- get your partner to bring you a cup of tea and a biscuit *before* you get out of bed in the morning
- eat little and often
- avoid spicy foods and anything fatty
- eat more wholewheat bread, lentils and other pulses, fish, chicken and other bland but nourishing things.

However sick you feel, it won't affect the baby. Indeed, there is some evidence to suggest that women who suffer badly from sickness during pregnancy have particularly healthy babies! It is most important to ask your doctor or midwife if you have any worries at all. You may find this easier to do having found your way round the system before.

TESTS DURING PREGNANCY

Most hospitals now offer pregnant women at least one ultrasound scan to check that the baby is growing normally, and a blood test between sixteen and eighteen weeks which can identify spina bifida and some other problems.

If you are in your thirties, you may be offered additional tests with this pregnancy that you did not have the first time round. The risk of having a Down's Syndrome (mongol) baby increases with age, so older mothers are usually offered an *amniocentesis*. The age at which this becomes available depends on the local health authority's policy: some offer it to mothers who will be thirty-five or older when the baby is born, others restrict it to mothers over thirty-seven or thirty-eight. The National Genetic Foundation of the USA advises all women aged 35 or over to have an amniocentesis (or CVS).

An amniocentesis is carried out between fifteen and eighteen weeks of pregnancy. You are given a local anaesthetic and a very fine hollow needle is inserted through your stomach wall and into the womb, where it sucks out about half an ounce of the amniotic fluid in which the foetus is lying. Analysis of the fluid reveals if the baby is suffering from Down's Syndrome or certain other handicaps, such as spina bifida. It also reveals the sex of the baby.

Not everyone who is offered an amniocentesis accepts. Despite the local anaesthetic – which, of course, only affects the stomach wall – the procedure itself can be a bit painful. It also carries a risk of miscarriage. Some couples feel strongly that, even if the test reveals a defect, they would not consider an abortion anyway. Others prefer to have the test without being sure whether they would end the pregnancy or not.

You and your partner have to weigh up how important it is to you to have the baby tested. Obviously, your own age is an important factor: if you are forty or over, the risks of Down's Syndrome are much higher (see table below) and you may well feel that it is worth running the risk of miscarriage. But if you have found it very difficult to conceive, or have suffered previous miscarriages, any risk of miscarriage may not be acceptable.

Down's Syndrome in Babies	
Mother's Age	Incidence
35	1 in 365
37	1 in 225
39	1 in 140
41	1 in 85
43	1 in 50
45	1 in 32
47	1 in 20
49	1 in 12

(from Sheila Kitzinger, *Freedom and Choice in Childbirth*, Penguin, 1988)

There is now a new procedure – *chorionic villus sampling* (CVS) – which can be carried out as early as the ninth week of pregnancy. With this test, a tiny sample is taken from the chorionic villii (the minute protrusions on the outside of the fertilised egg, which enable the egg to implant itself in the mother's womb and which later form the placenta). The procedure is similar to an internal examination, with an instrument inserted through the vagina. When the test is carried out later in pregnancy, a needle is inserted through the stomach wall, as for an amniocentesis and a local anaesthetic is given. An ultrasound scan is used to ensure that the needle is guided into the right place.

Detailed laboratory investigation of the chorionic villii sample is then carried out. It usually takes a fortnight to get results, although if a sufficiently large sample is obtained, the analysis may be done more quickly. An abnormality can be detected, and an abortion offered, much earlier than with amniocentesis.

Like an amniocentesis, CVS is uncomfortable and can be painful. There is also a risk of miscarriage. Initially, it was feared that CVS carried a higher risk of miscarriage than amniocentesis. The initial report of a Canadian controlled trial suggests the risk may be slightly higher with CVS. In the Canadian trial, which began in 1984, nearly 3,000 pregnant women aged thirty-five or older were randomly allocated either amniocentesis or CVS. The study followed each woman throughout her pregnancy, collecting detailed information about the test results, the progress of the pregnancy and the outcome. (The results of a similar national trial in Britain will be available later in the year.)

The Canadian study found that both groups of women suffered a *total* loss rate – miscarriages, abortions and stillbirths – of around 7 per cent. Within this total figure, women in the CVS group were slightly more likely to give birth to a stillborn baby. Researchers have not yet arrived at an explanation for this difference. Those who had CVS, perhaps not surprisingly, were also more likely to experience bleeding and 'spotting' than the other women.

Fears have also been expressed about the rate of 'false positives' from CVS. A 'false positive' means that, although the CVS analysis shows a chromosome abnormality, a later amniocentesis shows that the test result was wrong. In a very few cases, where an abortion has taken place, analysis of the foetus revealed the error.

Doctors involved in the British trial now believe that, provided all the cells obtained in the CVS show an abnormality which is known to occur in abnormal but live-born babies, then the chances of the result being a 'false positive' are tiny. It is also possible for CVS analysis to reveal a chromosomal abnormality that has never been reported in a live or stillborn baby. If this happens, and the scan shows the baby growing normally, then the doctors would strongly advise an amniocentesis rather than a termination.

The problem arises where only *some* of the cells from the CVS reveal an abnormality. If the normal cells are female, further analysis is done to ensure that these really are the baby's cells, and not the mother's.

If you have the misfortune to be given an adverse result from a CVS, you will of course need to discuss it fully with your doctor. Where the result is uncertain, for the reasons just explained, then you may well prefer to wait for an amniocentesis rather than decide on an early termination.

Sometimes, CVS fails to produce a result either way – either because it proves impossible to get a sample, or because of problems with the laboratory analysis. In such cases, a follow-up amniocentesis would be recommended. Waiting for an amniocentesis means, of course, that you lose the advantage of an early diagnosis *and* you have several weeks' more worry. But the chances of this happening are small enough not to outweigh the benefits which CVS offers.

CVS is not yet available throughout the country. If you *are* offered it, you and your partner will need to weigh up the advantages and disadvantages of the test and discuss them with your doctor.

DO YOU WANT TO KNOW THE BABY'S SEX?

Both CVS and amniocentesis reveal the baby's sex. Some hospitals and doctors have a policy of not telling the parents this information, usually because they fear that some parents may decide to terminate a pregnancy if the baby is the 'wrong' sex. (Of course, no abortion could legally be carried out for this reason.) This raises an important ethical question about whether doctors should withhold information which directly affects you, or whether you should yourself decide whether or not you want to know.

Some doctors will tell you if you ask, or if you argue hard enough, as Joanna found out:

> The doctor was quite reluctant to tell me – she seemed to think it would spoil the birth if the sex wasn't a surprise! I explained that we'd both thought about it a lot and that knowing now wouldn't spoil anything – it would just increase the pleasure of the pregnancy, knowing the sex of the child we were going to have. So she did tell me.

One of the fathers we spoke to found it very helpful to know the baby's sex in advance: 'It helped me to make contact with my baby beforehand. Knowing she was a girl made her more real during the pregnancy. It was easier to find a name for her too!'

A lot of people feel, however, that you're 'spoiling the surprise' if you know in advance. If you choose to be told the sex, and then tell other people, you may find they're quite shocked or disapproving.

Other parents, like Mary, would prefer not to know:

> I longed for a girl this time but I was convinced it was a boy. I knew I'd love the baby when he was born, but I thought if I knew in advance it would just upset me all through the pregnancy and might make it more difficult when the baby was born. So I was very grateful when the doctors didn't even mention it. In fact, it was a girl.

TELLING YOUR OLDER CHILD

Most parents don't tell their older child immediately they find they are expecting another baby. After all, it's a long time for the child to wait before the baby arrives. And if the child isn't talking yet, you may feel that it's difficult to explain. Even a very young child, however, may understand a great deal more than you realise, particularly if she can't put it into words. And it is obviously far better that she hears about the new baby from you, instead of being told by a visitor or piecing together overheard conversations. You and your partner will need to decide the best time for you and your child.

Chris explained that she and Joe decided to wait until she was already quite large before telling Robert, who was not yet three, about the new baby:

> He was having a bath with me one evening and I asked him whether he'd noticed that my tummy was getting bigger. I explained there was a baby growing inside there. He got quite interested and decided he was growing a baby in his tummy too. After that he talked about it occasionally, but didn't seem overinterested – although we heard from other families he played with that he often told them he was going to have a baby.

If you and your partner have been told your baby's sex, you'll also have to decide whether to tell your child too. Since you'll be talking about the baby as 'he' or a 'she', it makes sense to explain to your child that she will soon have a brother or sister. If you think the other families she plays with, or her grandparents or other relatives, will react badly to your child's announcement of the baby's sex, you may need to warn them first!

Penelope Leach recommends getting your child used to the idea of brothers and sisters by making sure that she meets families with several children. There may be a very new baby in the neighbourhood whom she can meet and be helped to cuddle. You can talk about her friends' brothers and sisters. If you're having an ultrasound scan, you could ask the hospital whether they can provide a photo of the baby from the scan, to share with your child.

Once you've told your child, you may find her getting very interested in babies and excited about the idea of having a new baby at home:

> Sally was only a year old when we began introducing her to the idea of a younger brother and of course she didn't have the words to talk about how she felt. But we did notice that she paid a great deal of attention to a friend's baby who spent quite a lot of time with us. She would shriek with excitement when they arrived and try to crawl into the crib with him.

If your child does respond like this, encourage her by talking about the baby, asking her how she thinks the baby feels, showing her how the baby has her nappy changed and so on. As we explain later (see page 47), one of the most important ways you can encourage a good relationship between your own children is to talk about the new baby as a person from the start. So it makes sense to get her used to treating babies as people too!

TAKING YOUR CHILD TO ANTENATALS

If you are a full-time mother, you may have no choice about taking your child with you to antenatal check-ups. Or if your child is very interested in the idea of a new baby, you may choose to involve her in this way.

Some doctors and hospitals provide excellent facilities for children. Others don't. Either way, it's sensible to go well-equipped with juice or milk, books and one or two favourite toys to help entertain your child. Talk to your child about the other children there who are also going to have new brothers or sisters, and the other mothers who are going to have babies.

YOUR CHILD WAS A BABY TOO!

These months of waiting are a good time to remind your child that she was a baby too. Bring out the photos of her birth and first few weeks. Tell her about some of the things *she* did as a baby – like sucking on mummy's breast or screaming all throught the night – and talk to her about what the new baby might do. Explain that the new baby won't be able to do all the things she can now do, like feeding herself or using a potty.

You might want to make a scrapbook with your child, or find pictures about babies to put up on the wall. It's all part of helping her to understand that having a brother or sister is something that happens to lots of people, and that the new baby will be a person with likes and dislikes, just like her. But remember, too, that a lot of time she feels that *she* is the baby and she will be upset by the idea that there's only room for one baby in the family. So don't push too hard the idea that she's a 'big girl' now. If she wants to be cuddled like a baby, or to lie down in the baby's carrycot, let her.

RESPONDING TO YOUR CHILD'S DISTRESS

You may be lucky enough to have a child who reacts calmly or with positive pleasure to the idea of a new baby. But most children will have mixed feelings – excitement at the prospect of a newcomer, fear that you no longer love her enough, resentment at the change to her settled life. Some children will show their anger even before the baby is born, as Mary found:

> I couldn't believe it when Robert started hitting me in the stomach. He was only about fourteen months old and I wasn't even sure he'd understood when we explained that we were going to have another baby. But he certainly did understand, even though he couldn't talk about it himself – and he was really furious. Of course his routine was disrupted. I was exhausted, and I'd sometimes come home and go straight to bed while his father looked after him. And as I got bigger, I couldn't romp with him as much. I tried to show him how the baby was in my tummy, but instead of feeling my tummy he'd hit it!

If your child reacts like this, you're bound to be very distressed. If you're delighted about the new pregnancy, then you want your child to share your pleasure. And if you're worried about being pregnant again – perhaps because the pregnancy was an accident – then your older child's distress can only make things worse.

Try to imagine how your child is feeling. Several baby books compare the child who is told that a second baby is on the way with a wife whose husband announces that he's going to bring a second wife home. It may sound reasonable to say to the child: 'We love you so much we want to have another baby', or 'Won't it be nice for you to have another baby to play with?' But how would *you* feel if your partner said: 'I love you so much I want to have another wife', or 'Won't it be nice for you to have another wife to talk to?'

The comparison may sound far-fetched. But the distress and anger which some children experience does suggest that they feel just as bitterly hurt as the woman whose partner walks out on an apparently happy relationship. The first-born child has had her parents to herself for the whole of her life. *You* may have planned a larger family from even before she was born, but she doesn't know that. As far as she's concerned, the secure world which you have built around her is changing. And even for most adults, change can be very hard to cope with.

It may be hard, but it's actually a good sign that your child can express her distress so openly. It's worth reminding yourself that children who bottle up their feelings are much more likely to have difficulties later; anger and fears which have been hidden under a mask of independence and good behaviour may suddenly erupt in a really dangerous attack on the baby. By helping your child to handle her feelings, you are doing her a tremendous service.

Talk to your child about how she feels. Even if she can't tell you herself, it will help enormously if you can put her feelings into words. 'I know you're angry and upset because Mummy looks different. And you don't want Mummy to have another baby. You want to be the only baby. But you don't need to be scared.

Mummy and Daddy love you all the time. You'll always be our baby Ruth. But there's plenty of room for another baby.'

If your child does hit you, that must be stopped, of course. But try to find her some other way of letting off steam. Show her how to punch a cushion or a beanbag, perhaps saying 'Show me how angry you are' as you demonstrate.

Do try not to feel guilty yourself. If your child does react badly or seems rather sad, it's easy to overreact yourself. Look back on your own childhood. If you were the oldest child and were very jealous of a younger sister or brother, then you may be adding your own memories to your child's reactions. If you felt that your parents 'ruined your life' by producing another baby, you may be feeling very guilty about doing the same thing to *your* child. It should help to talk about these feelings and memories with your partner and to discuss his childhood experience too. It may help too to look at Chapter 1 of this book, to remind yourself of the enormous pleasures and advantages which your child can gain from having a new sibling.

But if you still feel distressed and are having trouble handling your child's reactions, do talk to your doctor, midwife or health visitor. They know that a second pregnancy can have its own problems, and this is one of them.

TIME WITH THE FATHER

One of the most striking findings of the Cambridge survey (see page 14) is that where the older child is close to the father *before* the second baby is born, difficulties and conflict between the child and the mother after the birth are less severe.

So now is the time to help your partner develop a really close relationship with your child, if it doesn't already exist. It's very important that the father should increase the time he spends with the child, perhaps developing a routine of regular Saturday and Sunday outings. If you have always put the child to bed yourself, it's a good idea to involve him now, by taking turns or sharing every bedtime. Or the father could take over bathtime. (See Chapter 5 for more on fathers.)

If the father puts in time *now*, then there's a very good chance that life after the new baby is born will be much easier. Once the baby is born, it's much more difficult since your child may feel she's being fobbed off with her father when the person she really wants is you.

HOME OR HOSPITAL?

Early in your pregnancy, you will have to decide whether to have this baby in hospital or at home. Unlike the first time, you will also want to take account of your older child's needs.

Having your baby in hospital means that you and your child will be separated, even if it is only for a few days. Your going away, and having other people helping to look after her as well as going to the hospital to visit you and to meet the new baby will all add to the disruption in your child's life.

On the other hand, you may feel safer with a hospital birth, or there may be medical reasons for giving birth in hospital. Some mothers feel they can get more rest in hospital than at home and will welcome the opportunity to get to know the new baby without the older child competing for attention.

If you do decide on a hospital birth, you should have some choice about how long you stay. If you want to get home as quickly as possible, the hospital will be most unlikely to object (unless, of course, there are medical reasons for either you or the baby to stay in longer).

Most hospitals expect second-time mothers to leave after forty-eight hours unless there are special reasons for a longer stay. If you want to, you can arrange for an even shorter stay. With the Domino scheme, you are looked after throughout your pregnancy by a community midwife who then goes into hospital with you to deliver your baby. If you want to, you can leave a few hours after the baby is born, or you can stay in hospital overnight. The midwife continues to look after you at home for the first ten days after the birth.

This arrangement suits many mothers who want the security of a hospital delivery in case something goes wrong but who also want to be away from home and the older child for as short a time as possible. If you are interested in a Domino delivery, ask your GP early on in your pregnancy if it is available locally.

When you are making the arrangements for your second baby, you may be particularly worried about the effect of your absence on your first child. But don't forget that you will need time with your new baby too, to get breastfeeding established and to get settled generally. Mothers having a third or fourth baby often seem to worry less about the effect on the older children and find reasons to stay in hospital and get a rest and time with the new baby.

Chris decided that she needed extra time to get to know her new baby and arranged to stay in hospital for three days.

> I just wanted this precious time alone with my new baby. It sounds awful, but Ruth's demands just seemed so intrusive and out of place that I felt I couldn't cope immediately with looking after her too.

WHILE YOU ARE AWAY

How your child reacts to this separation will depend very much on whether she has begun to get used to you being away, or whether this is the first time. A child whose mother went back to a full-time job after maternity leave will already be used to being looked after by a grandparent, childminder or some other carer: if the same person can take care of her while you're in hospital, then the separation may not feel too different.

If, on the other hand, you and your child have almost never been apart, even a short separation from you will be a disruption and you need to make the arrangements as carefully as you can. Obviously, the person who comes to look after her should be someone she already knows and trusts – a grandparent or close friend, for instance. You might want to arrange for the person concerned to come and stay some time before the birth, so that the baby's birth won't be the first time this visitor has stayed overnight. It is also a good opportunity to get the grandparent, or whoever it will be, used to the child's routine.

Even small changes can be upsetting for a child. So do make sure that whoever is coming while you are in hospital is filled in on the tiniest details of your child's day: favourite toys, the food she likes and dislikes, a special cup or spoon, and every step in the bedtime routine. Many mothers in the Cambridge survey emphasised the problems which the substitute 'mother' (including the father) unwittingly caused by simply not understanding how much small details of the child's routine contributed to her well-being.

As far as possible, it is also important to stick to whatever rules you already have about what is allowed and what is forbidden. Grandparents or fathers who overindulge a child, or who are stricter than you are, can make it more difficult for her to settle back down with you after you come home.

HAVING YOUR BABY AT HOME

Home births used to be routine, of course. And a growing number of women are now choosing to have their babies at home. You may feel that, having already had one baby, there is no particular reason to go into hospital and you would prefer to give birth in the comfortable, familiar surroundings of your own home. You may dislike the clinical atmosphere of the hospital and the association of such a normal process with illness and medical technology. If you want to have a natural birth, helped by a midwife and your partner or friends, home may be an easier place than a labour ward. And, of course, you may want to avoid separation from your older child.

Many doctors are reluctant to let first-time mothers give birth at home. If you would prefer a home birth, you are likely to find it much easier the second time round. Discuss it with your doctor as soon as you have your pregnancy confirmed. Your own GP may do home deliveries herself or, if not, be happy to refer you to a colleagues or a community midwife. If your doctor is unsympathetic, you could contact one of the organisations listed in Appendix II for help.

LETTING YOUR OLDER CHILD BE PRESENT AT THE BIRTH

Some parents feel strongly that they want the other child present when her baby brother or sister is born. Others hate the idea and are worried that the child will be upset.

Only you and your partner can decide whether your child should be around when the baby is born. Many psychologists feel that seeing and hearing the mother's pain is too distressing for a child who simply does not have the emotional equipment to handle the experience. Some report that women who are themselves pregnant suffer from the long-buried memory of hearing their own mother give birth to a younger sister or brother.

There is also the practical problem of looking after the child while you and your partner concentrate on getting the baby born. One midwife told us about a couple who insisted on having their eight-year-old daughter in the labour ward. When the child became bored, the father took her for a walk, much to the distress of the mother who angrily demanded that he return to look after her during a painful contraction.

Most hospitals are reluctant to allow an older child into the labour ward. A good compromise may be to arrange for the child to be brought to the hospital immediately after the baby is born. Your child can still share those wonderful early moments with you, but your midwife will have time to deliver the afterbirth and clean up after the labour.

If you would like your child present or nearby during the birth, then this is an additional reason for having the baby at home. An older child may also find the experience easier to cope with. This is how one mother, whose four-year-old and seven-year-old boys were both present at the birth of their baby sister, described the experience:

> One night, after their bedtime story, we talked a little about our coming baby. They were wondering what would happen to them on the day the baby came. I had already arranged a home birth and was about five months pregnant by this time. Quite spontaneously they then asked if they could be there at the birth. I was taken aback slightly, but promised to discuss it with daddy. His immediate reaction was, 'Yes, what a good idea.' We decided to let them be as much involved as possible, so from then on we looked at books, watched any helpful TV programmes, and did lots of talking about how babies are born, without romanticising the subject...
>
> Much to my surprise, the midwife was in favour so long as everything went well and we had someone here to look after the boys. So we lined up Stephanie (a close friend) to help out...
>
> The boys were wonderful; they ran errands, rubbed my back while James, my husband, was supporting me during contractions, took phone calls, and finally they were just sitting there. I made rather a lot of noise in the second stage, but it only lasted one minute so it was soon over, and they were thrilled and awed to have a new sister...
>
> The boys were fascinated by the afterbirth and asked to look at it.

They will not need to ask where babies come from!
(*Giving Birth: How it Really Feels* by Sheila Kitzinger.)

As this mother and her midwife realised, it is essential to have another adult to care for the older child or children so that you, your partner and your midwife can concentrate completely on the birth. If the other child gets bored or distressed, it's obviously much easier to find other things for her to do if you're giving birth at home instead of in a hospital labour ward.

PREPARING FOR THE BIRTH

Your second baby's birth may be very different from your first. If you had a long, and perhaps difficult labour the first time, then it's a relief to know that second labours are almost always shorter, simply because the body's tissues are softer and adjust more quickly to the birth process.

You'll find it useful to go back to the pregnancy books or notes which you used for your first baby, to remind yourself of the different stages of labour. But just because it's different, you can't rely on what you learnt in your first pregnancy to see you through this time. Your hospital, health centre or local National Childbirth Trust should offer special classes for mothers having second or subsequent babies, and it's a very good idea to attend if you possibly can. You should also go on the tour of the hospital maternity wing if this is offered: routines and layout can change very quickly.

If you're having a second or later child after a gap of several years, you'll find that hospital procedures have changed enormously. Most hospitals have abandoned the enema and shaving which used to be compulsory. Partners are not only allowed but enthusiastically encouraged to help with the birth. And many hospitals are happy to try and meet the wishes of women who want to have a natural birth, actively moving about during labour, perhaps being able to have a bath or use a birthing chair, doing without drugs for pain relief and so on.

Deidre Jameson, the senior obstetric physiotherapist, and Adrienne McMeeking, the senior midwife for parenthood and health education, give refresher classes at University College Hospital, London. They are convinced of the special value of classes for mothers having a second, third or later baby:

> Pregnancy the second time round is often *harder*, physically and emotionally. You're more tired and there's no time to think about yourself or the baby. A lot of women say to us: 'I just haven't thought about this pregnancy.' Even two two-hour classes – which is what we offer – gives the mothers time to think and tune in to this pregnancy.

Another value of the refresher class is that it gives you a chance to work through your feelings about your first labour. Deidre Jameson says the classes are 'like a cushion for women who may have had a very painful experience the first time round. The other women are very sympathetic and a mother who perhaps hasn't talked to anyone about what she went through before finds it's safe to let her feelings out, to cry if she wants to.'

PREGNANCY, PREPARATION AND LABOUR

If you had a difficult labour previously, it is very important to get reassurance, as Shirley found. She had a long and difficult labour with her first child, only partly helped by an epidural. It took her a considerable time to get over the experience, although once she was pregnant with her second baby she was able to look forward more confidently to the birth.

> The first time was terrible. I still can't talk about it properly. I was quite angry that no one warned me, and the books gave no idea that things could be so bad. I was amazed I could let myself get pregnant again and face another birth. But actually the memory didn't affect me much during pregnancy. I knew it wouldn't be the same and my consultant just kept telling me it would be a breeze!

Mothers who are pregnant for the second time are sometimes unwilling to talk in front of women who have not had children, or who are in their first pregnancy. If you've had a very difficult first birth, you may well be reluctant to frighten another woman with your experience. That is why classes for first-time mothers should be kept separate and medical students should not be brought into the refresher classes.

It is also a good idea *not* to try and take your older child with you to one of these classes. Other mothers may be reluctant to talk about a painful first labour with a child present, and you won't want your child overhearing something which may be even more frightening because it is only partly understood.

WHAT YOU NEED IN HOSPITAL

Another reason for going to refresher classes – or at least on the hospital tour which is usually offered to pregnant women – is to check up on what you need to take into hospital. Hospital policy can change surprisingly fast. As with your first baby, you need to have your bag ready a week or two before the baby is due.

GOING INTO LABOUR

With a first baby, it can be quite difficult to know whether you're really in labour or not. You may have 'false starts' or the contractions may build up very slowly, over several hours or even several days as the cervix begins to dilate. With a second baby, the start of labour is often much more obvious – and things can move surprisingly quickly.

The usual signs that labour is starting are:

- A 'show' – a blood-stained mucous discharge.
- Your waters break.
- Contractions start.

Once any of these things happen, you should contact your midwife or the hospital *immediately*. They may advise you just to carry on at home, but if you're having a hospital birth, you may be advised to come in straight away to avoid the risk that the baby will suddenly be born in transit.

With a second baby, it is very easy to remember how slowly things progressed the first time round and assume that you've got plenty of time even after contractions start. But things are different this time, whether your first baby was eighteen months or eighteen years ago. Because your tissues are softened from the first birth, your cervix should open far more easily and quickly than it did the first time. Contractions, too, are more efficient with a second or subsequent labour. That is why it is not uncommon for a second-time mother to go from 2 to 8 cm in half an hour.

If you had a very long or difficult labour with your first baby, the thought of a shorter labour is likely to be a great relief! But a short labour has its own difficulties. It can feel bumpier, much rougher and, because the pain doesn't build up so gradually, the contractions may suddenly become overwhelming. It helps a great deal if you and your partner are prepared for this.

Most first labours progress in a fairly gentle, straight line, with the contractions gradually becoming more and more painful and the cervix gradually opening to the full 10 cm. With a second or later baby, the shape of the labour is more like a series of steps: you may stay at, say, 3 or 4 cm for a while and then suddenly, after one or two contractions, open to 6, 8 or even 10 cm.

If you have an experienced midwife, she will understand the feeling that your labour may suddenly have 'changed gear'. But you may find that you're still in the antenatal ward when your contractions change intensity and become much more demanding and urgent. Or you may have been examined only an hour or so ago by a midwife who found that you were only 2 or 3 cm dilated and who is reluctant to examine you again so soon. You will need to insist that your labour *has* changed, that things are moving fast and that you should be moved to the labour ward or examined again.

Carol found the speed of her second labour very frightening:

> I came into hospital to be induced, because the baby was thirteen days overdue. I had a pessary first thing in the morning, and then another at lunchtime because things weren't progressing. By 4 o'clock I was getting exhausted, and I was very depressed when the midwife examined me and said I was still only 4 cm. She went away and left Roger and me to it. Then I suddenly got this overwhelming urge to go to the toilet, to open my bowels. I simply didn't realise that this meant the baby was ready to be born and I needed to push: with my first baby, I had an epidural and a forceps delivery, so I didn't feel the urge to push at all.

Unfortunately, Carol's midwife didn't recognise what was happening either:

> Then the sister came in and I told her what was happening. She got angry with the midwife for not having given me an enema and sent her off for a bedpan! I told her again I wanted to push, and she said: 'Urge to push, nonsense! You're only 4 cm!' Roger and I just got more and more frightened because we didn't know what was happening. I was in real pain and I was still lying curled up on the bed – if I'd known the

baby was about to be born I'd have moved into a more comfortable position. The sister went out to get the midwife back, and then Roger and I could see the baby's head, and I screamed – and the sister came back and finally realised the baby was being born.

As Carol found, a second-time mother can go from first to second stage very quickly. If you feel an urge to push, or you feel that the baby is coming, then it is very likely that your cervix is fully dilated and the baby is indeed ready to be born. Again, an inexperienced midwife may find this hard to believe – especially if you were only 2 cm dilated an hour or so ago! But a midwife who is attuned to the differences with a second or subsequent labour may herself spot that you have suddenly gone into second stage, as your breathing or cries change in response to a particularly intense contraction.

Adrienne McMeeking at University College Hospital described one mother who had no preparation for her second labour and who found she simply couldn't cope with the unexpectedly strong contractions.

> Her husband assumed she was in the early stages of labour and kept telling her to pull herself together! She said she felt as if she was dying, she hadn't had anything like this with her first baby. Nobody believed her when she said how hard the contractions were. Then a senior nurse arrived who realised she had gone into second stage, and told her to shut her mouth and push. After that, the mother felt she was in control and things were fine.

Telling someone to 'shut her mouth' may sound brutal: it's actually good advice when you're ready to push your baby out and need to use your energy for that, not for screaming.

With a first baby, the second stage as you push the baby out can be very slow, hard work as the baby's head pushes down against your pelvic floor, slipping back a little after each contraction. Forceps, or a suction device called a 'ventouse', are often used to keep the baby's head down after a contraction. With a second or later baby, your pelvic floor tissues are so much softer that the baby's head doesn't slip back. The birth is faster and you are much less likely to need a forceps delivery or stitches.

PAIN RELIEF THE SECOND TIME ROUND

The speed of a second labour can also make it difficult to get pain relief in time. You may, for instance, be planning to have an epidural for pain relief.

An epidural is an anaesthetic injected into the outside part of your spinal cord and designed to remove all sensations from your waist down. You remain completely conscious throughout, although you do have to stay lying down. While the anaesthetist is inserting the epidural, you have to lie on your side, legs curled up to your stomach.

An epidural can only be given while you are in the first stage of labour. With a first baby, there is usually plenty of time for you to decide, as the contractions become painful, that you want an epidural and for the anaesthetist to give it. In a second labour, you need to make the decision very early on, as Joanna describes:

> I had an epidural with my first baby and was very grateful for it. With my second baby, I thought I would see how things went. To start with, I found I could manage the contractions just by breathing. But then it got much more painful and I asked for an epidural. The anaesthetist came very quickly, but she had a bit of trouble getting the injection into my back. Then I had a very strong contraction, and suddenly my midwife said: 'You're in second stage.' The anaesthetist stopped what she was doing, packed her bags, said 'Best of luck' and disappeared! I nearly panicked, but my midwife was wonderful, got me off the bed and I gave birth naturally using a birthing stool, supported by my husband and a medical student.

If you are certain that you want an epidural, you need to ask for it very early on even though the contractions at that stage may be bearable.

The same applies to pethidine, which is a narcotic widely used to take the edge off the pain of labour. Particularly if you found that the contractions made you very tense in your first labour, you may find the pethidine helps relax you if it is given at the beginning of this labour. But pethidine does not take effect for fifteen minutes, so it will not help if you delay until the contractions become very painful.

Some women find that pethidine makes them 'woozy' or even nauseous. You may prefer to rely on breathing and, if you want it, gas and air, to see you through the contractions. If you didn't use gas and air in your first labour, you will find it helpful to practise using the mask at an antenatal class.

CAESAREAN BIRTHS

'Once a Caesarean, always a Caesarean' used to be the saying. If you had a Caesarean delivery with your first baby, you need to talk to your doctor about whether you can try to deliver your second baby normally or whether you will require a second Caesarean.

If your first Caesarean was needed because your pelvic passage is simply too small to allow a normal birth, then you will almost certainly need a Caesarean again. But if there was a different reason for the first operation – for instance, because the baby was breach or became distressed in labour – then there is no reason why you cannot give birth normally this time.

This is something you need to discuss with your midwife and consultant during your pregnancy. If you agree that a Caesarean is needed again, then it can be helpful to plan this in advance, and to arrange to give birth under an epidural rather than a general anaesthetic. With an epidural, you remain conscious throughout the birth, even though you have no sensation below the waist. And your partner can stay with you.

If you do have a Caesarean with your second baby, you will of course take longer to recover than if you'd given birth normally. Once you get home, you will need extra help for several weeks since you won't be able to carry your first child or pick up heavy bags.

3 The first year

INTRODUCING YOUR CHILD TO YOUR BABY

If you've had your baby in hospital, you'll probably want to bring your older child in to meet his new sister as soon as possible. He'll probably be very excited, especially if he's never been to a hospital before and if you've already told him what to expect about meeting a new baby. One child we know insisted on dressing up in her nurse's uniform for the occasion. Other children have been known to try to climb into the newborn baby's cot in their enthusiasm!

If baby give me this, where he get the MONEY for it?

Parents are often advised to provide a small present from the baby to the child. It's worth doing to help the child realise that the baby is another real person who will give as well as take. But don't expect too much interest, as one mother points out:

Sally was so fascinated by this tiny baby that she just ripped off the paper, glanced at the wonderful toy tractor inside and cast it aside!

And Mandy says that her older daughter, Sarah, aged just over two when Jenna was born, refused totally to be fooled by this 'trick':

'Don't be stupid, Mummy', she said to me. 'I know the baby hasn't been shopping to buy me a present 'cos she's been inside your tummy!' I felt rather mortified at the deception, but we did see the funny side of it.

Some parents we know take their older child out beforehand to choose a present for the new baby. This exchange of gifts is a nice way to introduce the child to the idea that the new-born baby is another child, too.

The most important thing is to remember that this is a very big moment for your child and you need to try to understand his feelings. Those feelings are often complicated and conflicting. For example, after a separation like this, a child may be delighted to see you again and may be cuddly or even clingy. But on the other hand, he may be far too interested in the baby to pay too much attention to you, or he may be resenting your absence. And his ambivalent feelings about the baby may make him quite hostile or angry towards you, as we will see later in this chapter.

So it's sensible to keep an open mind about the way this first meeting will go. Show him how thrilled you are to see him again. Tell him how much you love him and have missed him. Be affectionate and generous with your hugs and kisses. But if, on the other hand, he's only interested in the new baby, that's fine, too! It will be a good start to what you hope will be a close and loving relationship between your two children.

But should your older child be indifferent or hostile to the baby, don't try to force him to show interest or affection. Show him the baby and tell him her name, or if you haven't decided on one, explain this to him. It's best to be sensitive to his feelings and accept them without comment or judgement and simply give him as much attention as you can. If the baby is asleep, this is a good time to have a cuddle together and perhaps tell him a story, just as you would do at home.

If your second child has been born at home, then of course, the question of a separation from your older one may not arise in the same way as with a hospital delivery. Most parents having a home confinement do so partly because it means they aren't separated from the rest of the family. Many parents like to have older children around during the labour and, in a few cases, present when the baby is actually born, as we saw in the previous chapter.

Whether your child is present or not at the actual birth at home, the chances are that you will have been together most of the time, unless he has been sent away to be cared for by a relative or neighbour. So the suggestions for the first meeting with the baby in the hospital setting are just as relevant for a home confinement. Your older child, however, may not experience the same intensity of resentment about you going away, but other ambivalent feelings are just as likely to be around.

COPING WITH HOSPITAL VISITS

Some children are very distressed by visiting their mother in hospital, especially when it's time to go home. Others get tired or bored, or want to run around the ward, so there's a risk of disturbing the other mothers and babies. If this is the case, then perhaps it's best to keep visits short. Don't assume that your child has to come to see you once or twice a day when you're away. See how he reacts the first time and ask him whether he would like to come again.

It's common policy for most mothers nowadays to be in and out of hospital within two or three days, unless they've had a Caesarean or there have been other complications. So in most cases, one or two visits are likely to keep your older child happy until you return.

If you have to spend longer in hospital, however, you may feel it's more important to have your child visit you regularly. Arrange with your partner or whoever is bringing your child into the hospital to make sure they have a good supply of drinks, snacks, toys and books to help keep him amused.

FEEDING: BREAST OR BOTTLE?

One of the first decisions you have to make when your baby is born (if you haven't already made it), is whether you are going to breast- or bottle-feed. For many women, their past experience with a previous baby is enough to confirm their decision. If breastfeeding has been a positive and successful experience with the first child, the chances are that it will be the same with the second, too. And the overwhelming evidence is that breastfeeding is better for the baby, as long as there are no medical or emotional problems getting in the way. So if you enjoyed breastfeeding your first baby, there should be no reason why you shouldn't enjoy it with your second one.

A large number of women do choose to bottle-feed for a variety of reasons and most babies thrive just as well, it seems, as long as the mother is happy with the arrangement. Some choose to bottle-feed their first child after an unsuccessful attempt at breastfeeding which may come about as a result of poor support and advice from the hospital staff.

Early breastfeeding problems can in most cases be easily overcome. These include sore or cracked nipples, poor positioning of the baby at the breast, blocked milk ducks, engorgement and inflammation of the breast (mastitis). With proper help, most women can continue to breastfeed, even after temporary bottle-feeding for medical reasons, as the milk supply can be restarted.

When a mother has resorted to bottle-feeding a first baby because of a failure in her attempt to breastfeed, she may feel a strong desire to breastfeed the second baby to help make up for the missed experience the first time. So it's important to make sure you have the right kind of support and encouragement for breast-feeding, including your partner's.

Many fathers feel positive about breastfeeding, but some research has indicated that they may occasionally envy the closeness between mother and baby and can feel excluded from their relationship as a result. A certain amount of sexual jealousy towards their baby's 'ownership' of the mother's breasts is also quite common, although it may not often be openly acknowledged. It can seem as if the new baby has taken over his wife's body, so that he no longer has access to it sexually. And these feelings may be aggravated by his partner's tiredness and lack of interest in sex which is particularly common during the early weeks and months after the birth of the baby.

A final factor in some men's ambivalence about breastfeeding is embarrassment, especially in public situations, where a wife exposes her breast to the gaze of other people. And although most people are used to seeing topless women in tabloid newspapers and on some beaches around the Mediterranean, it's a different matter when your wife is the only woman in company where everyone else is fully clothed.

WILL MY OLDER CHILD BE JEALOUS IF I BREASTFEED?

Although it is widely believed that a child will be more upset by his mother breastfeeding the baby than if she bottle-feeds, the largest study carried out in Britain of families with new babies found this was not the case. The older children were often naughty or disruptive at feeding time. But, if anything, the behaviour was *worse* during bottlefeeding than during breastfeeding – possibly because the breastfeeding mothers seemed to take more trouble to provide books, drinks, games and a potty for the older child before starting to feed the baby!

So you certainly don't need to feel that you shouldn't breastfeed because it might upset your child. However, you might want to get your baby used to the occasional bottle, apart from the breast. This can be either your own expressed milk or formula milk, depending on what's right for you. The advantage of doing this is that your partner, or another adult, can feed the baby, while you look after your older child, so that you're not completely tied to the baby all the time.

Whether you choose the breast or the bottle, the important thing is to find ways of keeping your child occupied while you feed the baby. Indeed, one advantage of breastfeeding is that you can have one hand free to hold a book while you read to your child. And many breastfeeding mothers we know soon learnt the art of continuing to feed the baby while walking around.

'I used to find myself taking my toddler to the toilet with the baby clamped firmly to one breast,' said one mother. 'It may not have been hygienic, but it kept them both happy!'

Mandy's older daughter took to banging doors and shouting every time her sister woke up to be fed, making feeding times a misery. The solution, however, was simple. Mandy turned feeding times into a story time for her older child, so that her attitude was swiftly transformed. From then on, she could hardly wait for the baby to wake up to be fed as Mandy describes:

> The number of stories we got through during those months of breastfeeding was enormous and the reward at the time was often a croaky voice and weariness at reading the same nursery rhyme for the umpteenth time. But there were hidden dividends because she's

grown up to be a voracious reader as a result of all that reading at such an early age. And it's likely that her baby sister absorbed a great deal of language, too, while still at the breast because she is also an avid reader.

WHEN IS THE RIGHT TIME TO WEAN YOUR FIRST CHILD?

One increasingly common practice among breastfeeding women is to delay weaning until the baby seems ready. Years ago, it was usual for weaning on to solids to start as early as four to eight weeks, although this is now strongly discouraged by most authorities. So now the earliest time mothers are advised to start the baby on solids is around three to four months in most cases, with milk as the main food until then. Yet there's no need to stop breastfeeding simply because a baby is eating solid foods and in many other countries it's quite normal for it to continue until the second or third year.

'Baby-led weaning' as it's called, is becoming increasingly popular in this country, largely because of more education and knowledge about breastfeeding and its advantages and also because of the greater acceptance of breastfeeding as a result. Many women are much more relaxed about feeding their babies than their mothers were and feel less inclined to stop the breast because of other people's opinions. The result is that it's quite common to see toddlers being breastfed occasionally, particularly for comfort and at night-time when settling down to sleep.

Mothers in this situation tend not to produce much milk as the supply regulates itself according to the relatively limited demand of the older child. So breast milk at this age is comparatively unimportant from a nutritional point of view to the older child, assuming that he is eating from a normal range of solid foods. And as long as everyone is happy with this arrangement, there's no harm in it. Most youngsters give up this kind of breastfeeding when they're ready as part of their own process of maturing.

TANDEM FEEDING

Worries do, however, crop up when a woman becomes pregnant with her second baby and is still feeding her first. Some women are concerned about the difficulty of breastfeeding during a second pregnancy, but the evidence is that as long as they are fit and healthy, there's no reason why the feeding should stop.

These worries may increase when the baby is born and the older child shows no sign of losing interest in the breast. So the result is that a mother is feeding two children at once – in which case it is known as 'tandem feeding'.

From a medical point of view, it's worth remembering that tandem feeding is very common in many other countries and women don't seem to suffer from it. As long as the mother is healthy and well nourished and has enough milk for her two children, there's no special reason to stop breastfeeding the older one. There is very little difference, after all, between feeding first and second children more or less simultaneously, and breastfeeding twins or triplets, which many women also succeed in doing.

However, if you are feeding an older child and want to try weaning, it's important to choose the right time. So for example, it makes sense to wean some time before your second baby is due, or else to delay it until some time after the birth. It can cause problems to stop your older child from breastfeeding around the time of the new baby's arrival, for the simple reason that he will probably be feeling quite jealous enough anyway. To attempt to stop an important source of comfort at such a critical and stressful time for your older child and to allow the new baby access to that comfort seems unfair and is likely to cause more conflict all round.

Choosing the right time to wean your older child depends partly on how often he is breastfeeding and how much solid food he is taking. A one-year-old, for example, may still be quite dependent on breast milk – much more so than, say, a two-year-old, who may be feeding for comfort before falling asleep. So timing the weaning is critical in the case of the one-year-old and you may need to allow much longer to wean him off the breast than for an older child. So if you would like your older child weaned before the birth of the baby, it's a good idea to start early in your pregnancy, rather than leaving it until later, in case you run into unexpected setbacks in the weaning process.

There is plenty of support and advice for breastfeeding mothers these days in the form of self-help support groups, such as The National Childbirth Trust, La Lèche League and the Association of Breastfeeding Mothers. Organisations like these have a network of breastfeeding counsellors who can help with specific problems. They are available for personal contact or for support by telephone if you live too far away from your nearest counsellor. They also have lists of helpful leaflets on various aspects of breastfeeding and can recommend suitable books (see Appendix II).

YOUR CONFLICTING FEELINGS

Your child is not the only one who may be feeling ambivalent about the arrival of the new baby. You, too, will probably be experiencing a storm of emotions that may be hard to sort out, depending on your personal circumstances.

In the case of older mothers, for example, who may already have had one or two children and then become pregnant when their youngsters are teenagers, there's the question of the inevitable round of tasks associated with babyhood all over again.

It's quite common to hear other women saying, for example: 'I don't think I could go through all that nappy washing and so on all over again. I'm glad I got it out of the way when I had my two so close together. It may have been hard work but it was worth it for the freedom we have now.'

Some mothers find that it takes them quite a while to come to terms with the fact that their baby is not the sex they wanted, especially where they did not know the results of antenatal tests that diagnose the baby's sex. We looked at this in more detail in Chapter 1 and suggested ways of trying to come to terms with this problem.

But more common among mothers of second-born babies is the question as to whether they will ever be able to love this one as much as the first. One mother who fell in love at first sight with her first baby girl, had serious doubts as to whether she would ever feel as intensely and passionately about another child:

> I adored my first baby, even though she was very difficult in the early months and cried a great deal. But when my second little girl was born, I didn't have the same intense rush of feelings as the first time. And that made me feel very guilty. I was detached from her and didn't find her pretty. The first few days I spent trying to get to know her and cope with my older child, then aged two-and-a-half.
>
> But miraculously, within a few days, all these doubts disappeared and I found myself just as loving as I had been before with the first baby. And she was a much easier baby, too, with a placid, sunny temperament. It was that experience which helped me realise that love isn't a finite object you have to limit or spread around carefully. It's much more a question of the more you love, the more love you have to give to others.

GETTING TO KNOW YOUR NEW BABY

It's generally assumed that mothers find everything much easier with a second baby – and indeed there is no mystery about the nappy-changing, feeding and bathing side of things. But your second baby may have a very different temperament and this can take you by surprise if you're not expecting it.

The baby may be easier (and some people do believe that second-time mothers tend to be more relaxed and therefore the second baby is often more relaxed, too). But it doesn't always work like this, as Joanna found:

> Katie was one of those dream babies who took to breastfeeding, slept peacefully and was happy to lie in her crib and look at the world. Robert, my second, was a nightmare – or that's how I felt! He never really took to breastfeeding and didn't gain weight well. My milk supply suffered and I gave up feeding much earlier than I wanted to. He just seemed to cry all the time and it was months before I felt he'd settled.

You need to give yourself time to get to know your new baby. Don't assume that what worked for your first one will necessarily work for the second. And if there's anything you're worried about, it's a good idea to talk to your midwife, health visitor or GP.

FAVOURING ONE CHILD IN THE FAMILY

But it's also true that parents do have their individual preferences and favourites among their children and they often feel bad or guilty about acknowledging such feelings, especially if they were aware of a favoured child in their family when they were young. Then the pressure is about loving the children 'equally'. But even in the most loving families, it's not possible to love each member identically.

If you think back to your own childhood and were lucky enough to have loving parents, it's unlikely that you loved your mother and your father identically, even though you loved them both. And it's the same with children: parents may be partial to one or another, and this partiality may change at different stages of their growing up, too. A child who is favoured as a baby may be supplanted by a sibling who becomes the favoured one during the teenage years. The problem is not so much that one is preferred, but that this preference is obvious to the other child who needs to be protected from feeling discriminated against by his parents.

One solution to this tricky but impossible question of trying to love children equally is instead to think of loving them uniquely. This means looking at each child as a special person, with his or her own unique qualities (and faults) which we value for themselves. So your feelings for your second baby may never be quite the same as for your first, but if this happens, don't blame yourself. Instead, remember that this child will also reveal characteristics that are lovable or of value to you later on and that you have plenty of time to get to know each other.

Mary described how she copes with this question as a mother of five sons:

> I don't think it's a question of loving your children 'equally'. I mean, you either love them or you don't. You love them because they're your children. That level of affection, the panic you feel if one of them is ill or unhappy is exactly the same for all of them. I think you respond to them as individuals because they *are* individuals. Sometimes, when I tick them off, and the message comes back 'You don't love me', I always say 'I love *you*. I don't love the things you do sometimes, but that's quite different.'

During the first few days after you have come home from hospital with the new baby, remember that your first-born will be going through an enormous readjustment to this new member of the family. It's you he wants most of all after all – you've been away for several days perhaps and now you're back and he has to compete with this tiny screaming bundle that everyone is fussing over.

If you have visitors, ask them to remember your older child, if they're bringing a gift. It's unfair to shower gifts on a baby and to expect an older child not to feel left out or that he's no longer the favourite. And ask them to give him plenty of attention, too, by saying 'hello' first to him before greeting the baby, and making sure that they talk to him about things he's interested in, and not just his new sibling.

Because new babies are very effective in making their needs know by crying, it's tempting to put them first. But if your older child sees you constantly attending to the baby first and putting him second, this only fuels his resentment and encourages his belief that you prefer the baby to him now. So try to make sure that you put him first at times, too. Ask your partner to look after the baby while you attend to him. And avoid the trap of expecting your partner always to look after the older child while you make the baby's needs your main task now. This will only make him feel he no longer has access to you. Try to share the care of both children with your partner – apart from anything, it will help your first-born to learn from an early age that men are just as good at parenting as women are!

Brenda describes how she realised that her older child needed *her* attention after she came home with her second baby:

> For the first month after I came home, I made sure Richard was looked after by someone he knew so that I could concentrate on the baby. Matt was home for the first week, then my mother came. Next I went to stay with her and took the children with me, and then my sister came to stay. At the time, I thought this was fine – he was being looked after by someone he knew. What I didn't realise was that he wanted *me* to look after him, and I think that contributed to him feeling excluded.

If your child is already close to his father before the new baby is born, this should help to reduce the conflict afterwards. But it's very important to get a close relationship established before the birth. If your child has seen little of his father before the baby arrives and is then suddenly expected to spend a lot of time with him while his mother cares for the baby, he is likely to feel resentful and excluded.

THE 'BABY BLUES'

During the first few weeks after the birth of your second baby, it's common to go through another bout of the 'baby blues', especially if they hit you the first time round, too. It's been estimated that up to 70 per cent of women go through some sort of low feelings or depression during the early postnatal period. (For more on postnatal depression see p. 58 in this chapter.) For most these only last a few days, or a couple of weeks, with lapses into crying or feeling overwhelmed by the responsibility of everything, or feeling isolated or alone in having to cope.

This depression, whether mild or severe, is usually attributed to hormonal changes in the mother as a result of the labour and delivery and it usually rectifies itself when the hormone system gets back into balance again. There are several ways you can help yourself to get through these low periods, even though they can seem endless during the early days.

The first thing to do is to remember to be patient with yourself and not to expect everything to fall into place at home immediately. You, your partner and your first child need time to get to know each other as a family of four now, with new demands and new pressures on your time. Most of your energy will be taken up with looking after the new baby – feeding, bathing, calming and trying to get extra rest to make up for the disturbed nights. Around this, you have to fit in many of your usual household tasks, so it's sensible to look at what doesn't need to be done at this time.

If possible, cut down on as much as you can so that you don't become overburdened unnecessarily. Make your meals simple and easy to prepare and keep your housekeeping chores to a minimum so that you don't get tired. Cut corners where you can by, for example, using disposable nappies, rather than terry ones, which means you have less washing and drying. Lower your standards to meet your needs now – you can always raise them again later on when you have more time and energy. Learn to ignore the dust, if possible, and leave the spring cleaning until next spring.

Avoid having too many visitors during the first weeks. Your friends and relations will want to see you and the new baby, but coping with too many at once, or too often, can be very stressful and means that you spend more time entertaining them than in looking after yourself. So don't feel guilty when you have to say no to a well-meaning friend or relative who wants to visit you to shower you with gifts and good wishes. Ask them to postpone their visit for a while until you feel able to cope and ask your partner to speak on your behalf if you don't have the strength to refuse. The best visitors bring you a ready-made meal, take your child for a walk and leave you in peace!

GETTING YOUR PARTNER'S HELP

If possible, arrange for your partner to take off as much time as he can from work after the birth of your baby. Paternity leave is still a long way off in Britain, although in most European Community countries and Scandinavia, fathers are officially recognised as playing an important part in the emotional and practical life of the young family. In many of those countries now, fathers are entitled to take time off from work when a baby is born so that they can take over some of their partner's work and get to know their own new-born child in peace and quiet, instead of having to rely on the odd hour or two in the evening and at weekends.

This may mean your husband having to take holiday leave in order to find the time to support you, but in the long run, it can be well worth it if his presence helps to take some of the pressure off you at home. And it gives him a chance to form a bond with your new baby, which otherwise might take a much longer time.

Research has shown that many fathers tend to feel excluded from caring for their young children, simply because of long working hours – particularly during the early years of marriage when money tends to be short and the cost of mortgages and establishing a home tends to be high. And these feelings of exclusion can be destructive to a relationship, because fathers may feel they have to compete with their own children for their partner's love and attention. (In Chapter 5, we suggest ways of dealing with these problems.)

But if your husband can't manage to be at home to support you, or if you're a single parent, it's still important to get help if you're feeling tired. It may be possible to organise other kinds of help, from say a neighbour or a friend who is willing to come and help look after your other child or take over chores like shopping or cooking, to give you a break.

EATING WELL

Looking after yourself when you're suffering from the 'baby blues' can seem difficult at a time of tiredness and listlessness. But it's especially important to keep your energy level up by eating well and making sure you're properly nourished, especially as your body will have been working overtime during the labour and delivery. This is important for you as well as the baby. You need a well-balanced diet of simple fresh food, with plenty of fruit, vegetables, whole grain cereals, and protein (such as eggs, cheese, pulses, nuts, and fish or meat).

Drink lots of fluids, especially if you are breastfeeding. Keep tea and coffee to a minimum and rely instead on fruit juices and bottled mineral water. Avoid processed foods as much as possible because so much of the nutritional value has often been lost during manufacturing and because so many of them have sugar, salt, fat and chemical additives to preserve their shelf life. And even if you don't feel much like cooking, it's not difficult to prepare salads and fruit dishes as the central part of your family's meals.

TALKING THINGS OVER

Apart from these practical strategies to help yourself, it's important not to bottle up your emotions when you're feeling down. If possible, find someone to talk to who understands what you're going through. This can be a woman friend or your health visitor, a sympathetic doctor, your own mother or mother-in-law.

Giving birth and bringing a new member into the family is an emotional time and it is a time to talk about your feelings, both positive and negative. Involve your partner in sharing your feelings, remembering that this is an emotional time for him too, and he may be going through all kinds of ups and downs in the process of adjustment. Don't feel that you have to keep everything to yourself in the belief that you're inadequate or failing in some way, because you're not coping as well as you hoped or expected.

So the more you can talk to one another, the closer you can build your relationship with each other. Being able to let off steam in this way acts as a safety valve so that you don't build up too much pressure inside yourself and let things get out of proportion for too long.

HELPING YOUR CHILD TO GET ON WITH THE NEW BABY

For many couples, the arrival of the second child is an occasion for celebrating. If you've planned to have just two – as many do nowadays – your family will be complete and you can look forward to your youngsters growing up happily together, as friends and companions for each other. Unfortunately, the reality is often not as simple as this, because of the problem of jealousy, which usually rears its head at some time or another. Most commonly, it is shortly after the arrival of the new baby and sadly, as many adults will confirm, can last a lifetime, with adult siblings still resenting and competing with each other.

Perhaps the most important thing that you can do from the baby's very first day is to talk to your child about the baby and help him to treat her as a real and separate person in her own right.

The study of families in Cambridge that we mentioned earlier (see p. 14) found that 'in families where the mothers discussed caring for the baby as a matter of joint responsibility and talked about the baby as a person from the early days, the siblings were particularly friendly over the next year'.

Brenda found that this helped when she was having problems with her older child:

> The problem was that Susie, the baby, just wouldn't feed if Richard was around – she'd get distracted and stop sucking. So I found increasingly I was saying to Richard: 'Would you mind playing over there?' and getting him to do something else, so that we were probably excluding him. And the time when I was most intimate with the baby I was pushing him away. But we only sat down and talked about this when Richard's behaviour became really bad and he scratched the baby a few times. Then we decided we'd have to encourage Richard to get more involved with the baby and give her bottles and help with nappies. We call her 'your sister' and he always says 'goodnight' to her. And gradually their relationship is growing!

As adults, most of us tend to like people who make it clear they like us. Exactly the same applies to your children. In these early months, when the baby can't make her own views known, you have a perfect opportunity to speak for her: 'Look, the baby's smiling at you. She likes you, doesn't she? Can you make her laugh? What happens if you tickle her toes?'

Try to keep up this line of chat whenever the two children are together. Research surveys do suggest that the more sociable the *baby* is, the better the older child will behave towards her. So it's worth encouraging and emphasising any signs of interest which the baby shows in her older sibling.

It also helps to involve your older child in caring for the baby. Even very young children can understand how a baby is feeling. Indeed, children are often very skilled and intuitive at telling parents exactly what a baby does or doesn't want!

You can encourage this by asking your child how he thinks the baby is feeling: 'Oh dear! The baby's crying. Do you think she's hungry? Maybe she needs a clean nappy? Shall we have a look?'

Burbling on in this fashion may sound silly, but remember there's no one else around to hear you – and in any case, you soon get used to it.

You can also encourage your child to help in practical ways. Even a very young child can help you find things you need, such as nappies, soap or baby cream, and he can splash water gently over her, talk to her or stroke her hands and so on. Obviously, you don't want your older child to feel resentful about being asked to help with the baby, however. So try to be alert to any signs that he really wants to be mothered himself.

You need to be ready to switch between asking him to help you and giving him the same treatment as the baby, if that's what he wants. One day, your toddler may proudly carry a toy or a bottle to the baby and get quite cross if you try to take over his responsibility. The next day, he may say: 'Feed me like a baby', and want you to spoon food into his mouth, or even cuddle him on your lap with a bottle.

Sharing the responsibility for the baby, and wanting to be just like the baby himself, are both entirely normal, healthy reactions. Don't try and force your child one way or the other.

JEALOUSY

Since jealousy is a fact of life in most families, what can parents do about it? It's tempting to pretend it doesn't exist or to wish it would go away or to get angry when the older child vents his feeling in a way that's unacceptable to you. But you need to remember that the arrival of a new baby is an enormous upheaval for your older child. For the whole of his life, he's had his father and mother to himself. Now, suddenly, there's another baby. It's not surprising if he feels that he wasn't good enough for you, or that you don't love him as much. He may become miserable and withdrawn, or angry with you or attack the baby. However he reacts, he's feeling something – and those feelings may be quite overwhelming for him.

As we've already seen in the previous chapter, it's wise to start preparing your older child for the arrival of the baby during your pregnancy. And this can be done, for example, by involving your youngster in things like helping to choose the new baby's clothes or any equipment or to help decide on what's needed for the baby's nursery, and so on.

But even the most thorough and sensitive preparation cannot prevent the powerful and turbulent storm of feelings your child will almost inevitably experience. And if you help your child to handle these feelings in a positive way you will also be helping him to cope with jealousy in the future. The idea of sharing your love and attention with another little stranger can be overwhelming for a first-born child. After all, he has had your undivided care for all his life and to see your time taken up so much in looking after the new baby means that he has less of you now.

It's wise to talk to your partner about your older child's reactions, as well as to anyone else who is involved with him or cares for him on a regular basis. Other adults can be very helpful in supporting a jealous child during these difficult early months and can give the extra attention you may not be able to provide just how because of the other pressures on your time. So do take up all offers of help, or ask for it if you need it.

Don't make the mistake, however, of fobbing your child off all the time with his father or another relative, either. Remember, your child needs *you*, too. It may be much better to ask someone else to look after the baby, while you have your older child to yourself for a while.

Interestingly enough, although the age gap between the children doesn't seem to affect the *strength* of the older child's reaction to a new baby, the age often makes a difference to the *way* the child reacts. So, for example, a very young child is more likely to become clingy and unhappy as a reaction, while a three- or four-year-old would probably become difficult or rebellious.

SLEEP PROBLEMS

It's very common for an older child to start having sleep problems or, if they already exist, for them to get worse, when the baby is born. Child psychotherapist, Dilys Daws describes in her book *Through the Night*, how a three-year-old started coming into his parents' bed after the baby's birth. He was so restless that he kept himself and his parents awake. The parents decided to keep him in his own room instead and explained that his father would come if he called, but he couldn't leave his bed. They promised him a small car as a reward.

After a few nights, he slept through the night and in the morning said to his father: 'You've been a very good boy. I shall buy you a new pair of cufflinks.' Dilys Daws comments that the boy's feelings of jealousy, which had been made worse by seeing the baby in his parents' room, had been helped by his parents' firmness in keeping him in his own bed. Luckily, sleep problems associated with the arrival of a new baby do seem to wear off after a few months.

SHARING HIS POSSESSIONS

Inevitably, you will want to use some of his former belongings for the baby and it's important to realise that he may still see these as his own. So he may be extremely attached to his former crib or cot, or his precious baby toys, or even his room from which he may feel ousted to make way for the unwelcome newcomer.

If possible, make sure he is given satisfactory replacements for these before you pass them on to his sibling. If the baby is going to take over her brother's cot, then it's a good idea to try to move him into his own bed before the baby is born. It's probably worthwhile repainting the cot so that it's not quite so obvious that his sister has moved into his own one. A new bed, a specially decorated bedroom or some 'grown-up' toys will help to soften the blow, especially if he has been involved in choosing them.

Parting with precious belongings is much easier when a child feels important and consulted about what's happening, no matter how young he or she may be.

If the new baby is going to share her brother's room, prepare him for this in advance. Even if your older child is very young and doesn't talk much himself, he'll almost certainly understand when you explain that his little sister is going to sleep in his room and show him where her cot will go and which blankets she will use.

The new baby will probably be inheriting some of his old clothes and baby toys. You could ask your child to help sort these things out and to choose things that his sister would like – or more cunningly, the things he doesn't want any longer!

You don't have to make too much of involving your older child in all this. But talking to him about everything that's happening, and warning him before things change will definitely make a difference. And discussing the new baby with him is one of the most important things you can do to help them get on together.

As the baby gets a little older, you may find your toddler wants to play with everything the baby shows an interest in. It's obviously not wise to let the child get the idea that he can take whatever he wants away from his younger sister. But constantly trying to get him to give the toy back to the baby may be too much to try to achieve. One compromise is to insist that if he wants to play with the baby's toy, then he ought to give her a substitute. This won't work in the case of older children, but you may find it a helpful strategy for a few months, meanwhile!

It can come as a shock to parents to realise just how intense the feelings of jealousy can be, and it's important to understand the different ways in which young children can express them. Not all of the following examples apply to every child, but some may show a combination of them.

DIFFICULT OR 'NAUGHTY' BEHAVIOUR

Even placid youngsters can become upset when threatened with a new baby and around 90 per cent display this kind of behaviour. Anger, hurt and resentment underlie it and it can appear in the form of deliberate disobedience and defiance to attract your attention when you're preoccupied with, say, feeding or bathing the baby. The remedy is to make sure that your child has something interesting to do while you're busy, such as a game to play, a picture book or television programme to watch, or a story to listen to. If feeding times, for example, seem to produce this kind of behaviour, then try turning them into a story time for your older child as well, as Mandy did earlier in this chapter. This can work wonders and turn a mini-nightmare of stormy behaviour into an oasis of peace in which the older child actually looks forward to the baby waking up!

Withdrawal and sadness

Some children become withdrawn or clingy after the birth of a sibling. This indicates that the jealous feelings are being contained inside your child and is common in youngsters who tend to be shy, quiet and introverted by temperament. For this reason, you need to be especially alert to the hidden feelings of rejection and isolation he is experiencing and to help him bring them into the open.

Calm and sympathetic acknowledgement, without undue exaggeration, will help your child to express what's going on for him. If he knows you understand how bad he's feeling and he feels reassured that you still love him just as much, you will go a long way to help him through this difficult and painful stage.

Small children find it difficult to express their feelings in words, because their language skills are not sufficiently well developed. It's very helpful, therefore, if you can put these feelings into words for your child as a way of showing that you understand what's going on inside him. This is an example of the kind of thing you can say: 'I think Tommy's very sad today. It's difficult having to share Mummy with another baby, isn't it? We all feel sad sometimes – children and grown-ups, too. I know how you feel...'

Avoid getting irritated at the clingy behaviour, if you can, and never blame him for how he's feeling. This kind of approach will only tend to reinforce the withdrawal and make him feel it's impossible for you to understand his deeper feelings.

It's easy to mistake a child who's quiet and withdrawn as one who simply isn't being any trouble to you, and therefore to overlook his or her unhappiness, especially if you're busy or preoccupied with other things. It may seem instead that he's coping very well – and this allows you to get on with dealing with the new baby. But according to the Cambridge study by Dunn and Kendrick, a child who is withdrawn or silent may become quite hostile and angry later on. So, for this reason, it's a good idea to deal with it sooner rather than later, and not to ignore it.

One of the remedies for this kind of reaction is to reassure your youngster with lots of attention and cuddles. This may not always be easy with the new baby around, but try to find time, perhaps when she's asleep or at bedtime when the two of you are on your own.

Regression

Many children show signs of regression when a new baby arrives. This means they revert to patterns of behaviour they had previously outgrown, such as wanting a bottle, or the breast, or to sleep in their cot again. Your child may start using 'baby talk', wet the bed, start soiling his pants or waking up at night. The logic behind this kind of behaviour is obvious enough. He sees the baby getting most of your attention, so the best way for him to get it is to be like a baby, too.

The remedy for this is not to get upset about these signs but to adopt a calm and patient approach. It's often easier to go with the babyish behaviour for the time being without attempting to correct it. You can gently point out what fun it is to be older and more 'grown up' and how many more things he can do that the baby can't because she's so young. Explain that as she gets older, she will also learn to be grown-up, just like him.

It's reasssuring to know that research has shown that children who do regress and imitate the baby are often friendlier to their siblings later on. So you can even encourage your youngster in this imitation, as it seems to be part of the process of helping him treat his sister as a real and different person.

But what do you do if your child wants to imitate the baby when she's breastfeeding? He may want to try sucking at your breast again, or he may try putting a doll or a teddy to his own breast. Some parents are in favour of letting a child try the nipple again, even if he's been weaned quite a long time ago. This could be embarrassing if the request comes up in public, but may be considerably easier to handle in the privacy of your own home.

Refusing to let your child try the breast again may make him feel excluded and jealous of the baby. So you may feel it's worth letting him try, as this mother did:

> Sally had stopped breastfeeding about six months before Richard was born. But when she saw him feeding, she became fascinated with my 'nibbles' – as she called them – and was always asking for a suck. It felt a bit funny, particularly as it went on for a while even after Richard had moved on to a bottle and there wasn't any milk left. And I had to explain to her that she wasn't allowed to bite! But I think it was good for her to know that she could still be a baby if she wanted to – and she gradually gave it up of her own accord.

Anger and aggressive behaviour

Your older child is angry. He doesn't want this new baby around – he wasn't asked and if he had been he would have said 'No' quite definitely. He didn't need a brother or sister – that was your idea, after all. So he's likely to want to hit or punch this unwelcome stranger, even though there may be times when he feels very loving towards her, too. And, of course, you have to protect the baby, which makes him even angrier and more jealous. Your immediate reaction to this kind of aggression is likely to be anger, as well, but unfortunately, this will only aggravate the problem. Your older child wants to know that he is still loved and is important to you and he needs this kind of reassurance desperately. Your job is to communicate that you understand his angry feelings, perhaps by saying that you would feel the same way, too, if you had to put up with all this disturbance and intrusion.

Sometimes the anger appears in the form of destructiveness, which means that it is being displaced on to other things and not the baby. Toys may be broken, books torn up or a favourite pet may be bashed, instead. Again, the remedy is to make a fuss of your older child and give him enough of your time and attention so that he doesn't feel neglected or left out. Encourage the anger to be expressed harmlessly, such as by punching a pillow or a soft toy, kicking a ball around out of doors, or suggesting he draws a picture of the baby that allows him to show how cross he's feeling. Try not to be shocked at what may come up when he does this, otherwise he'll become aware of your feelings of disapproval and will seek to avoid showing anger in the future.

Setting limits

At times like these it's useful to know how to set limits to angry, destructive behaviour. Keep your rules to a minimum, but be clear about what you regard as unacceptable. Anything that causes physical harm to you, the baby, your older child or to your home and belongings is in this category. If your child is behaving aggressively, you can try using what's known as the 'soft no'.

This approach is used when there's absolutely no room for negotiation or flexibility with your youngsters and you want to be firm but gentle in setting the limits he or she has to respect. You need to remain calm and clear about what you're insisting on and simply say something like: 'No, Timmy, you must not hit the baby. That is absolutely not allowed.'

If possible, sit or kneel when you say this so that you are at eye level with your child. Don't get angry or threaten, and if he resists, make your voice even quieter and firmer, instead of raising it. Don't offer explanations or justifications for the rule as this can get you drawn into an argument. Repeat the rule quietly and firmly as often as necessary and trust that your child will get the message, as long as you are congruent.

It may take a few occasions of this kind for him to understand that you mean business when you adopt this tone of voice, but gradually he will learn to respect that you mean what you say. The reason of course, is that it's very hard for anyone, adult or child, to escalate anger when the 'opponent' refuses to get drawn into the quarrel. And this approach is also very useful for dealing with all sorts of other situations particularly when your children are older.

Some parents find it very difficult to set limits on their children's behaviour. One child psychologist was approached by two distraught parents whose four-year-old daughter had been discovered holding her baby sister at the edge of an open window.

At the first visit, the mother sat down with the baby on her lap. The father and child took separate seats. As soon as the discussion started, the child made a beeline for her mother's lap and jumped on her knee, while the mother struggled to hold both baby and child. The psychologist told the mother to ask her child to return to her chair which she did grudgingly after four requests. The child then burst into tears, accused her mother of not loving her and insisted on sitting on her lap again. The mother gave in, looking rather guilty at the psychologist.

The psychologist concluded that the girl had become so used to 'getting away with murder' that she had very nearly murdered her younger sister. Once the parents learned to set limits on her behaviour, the baby was safe.

Attacking the mother

Your child feels rejected by you when you bring home the new baby. After all, you prefer her to him, so his reaction is to reject you. His pain is shown by attacking you, either physically, or verbally by complaining loudly to his Daddy or to anyone else who's around about how unfair you've been. This can be hard to deal with, when you've loved your older child so much and feel you don't deserve this kind of behaviour.

One mother we knew, Jenny, had quite a tough time with her older daughter, Bridget:

> Bridget started calling me 'the nipple'. She must have felt I never did anything except feed the baby! One day I'd popped out to the shops, leaving them both with their Dad. Someone phoned for me and Bridget, who was three then, answered the phone and said: 'No, you can't speak to her. The nipple's gone out!' It's still our favourite family joke.

Joanna found it particularly hard when her daughter rejected her after the new baby arrived, as she describes:

> For months after the baby was born, my daughter would take it out on me. If she cried out during the night and I went in to her, she'd scream to me to go away. 'I don't want you, I want my Daddy.' She'd get quite hysterical and refuse to let me give her a bottle or tuck her up.
>
> The same thing would happen in the morning when I went in to get her up. I became quite miserable and I'd often walk away from her or tell her not to be so foul. I talked to the health visitor about it and she said: 'Your daughter must be feeling really hurt.' And that made me realise that when she screamed at me, it wasn't because she hated me. It was because she was utterly miserable.

Try to put yourself in your child's shoes and see how you would feel if your husband brought home a new 'wife' one day, when you thought you had always been the most important person in his life. Looking at the problem from your older child's point of view can help you to understand how powerful his feelings of rejection are and will give you the patience to ride the storm without overreacting to it too much.

It can be very difficulties to deal with your child's anger towards you, especially if he becomes physically violent. Sometimes it can be helpful simply to turn round and walk away, while at other times giving extra attention to your child may be the right answer to the problem. You need to have a firm 'no hitting' rule, just as you do with the baby and with other children. But you also need to let him show his anger in other ways. So for example, you can help by saying something like:

> I think you're feeling very angry with me, aren't you, because I've got another baby now. That's OK – we all feel angry sometimes. You mustn't hit me but you can tell me how sad you're feeling.

One child we know used to express her feelings very firmly when she saw her mother holding the baby: 'Don't want two babies. Want one baby. Take him away,' she would say.

It helps a great deal to acknowledge her feelings:

> I know you don't want two babies. It's very difficult having to share your mother with another baby. But as soon as I've finished feeding the baby, we'll have a cuddle together – just you and me.

Another mother helped her child to understand his jealousy by cuddling him and saying things like:

> Are you my little jealous boy? Can I hug my jealous boy? Are you jealous all over. Is this a jealous knee?

Whatever words you use, helping your child to find words for his feelings and showing that you understand, makes a big difference, even if it takes time to work. It may be some comfort to realise that if he is taking his feelings out on you, he's probably less likely to attack the baby.

It's important never to underestimate the damage which an unhappy, angry child can do to a small baby. The older child's enthusiastic hugs may conceal real resentment as well as affection. Hostility doesn't always express itself in open blows – one child we know of was found 'posting' pennies into the baby's mouth!

One couple told us about the time their baby's finger was 'accidentally' jammed in a door, so badly that he had to be rushed off to hospital. When everything calmed down, the mother sat down with her daughter and asked how David's finger had been hurt. She was appalled to hear Julie say: 'Me no like David. Me put David's finger in the door. Me want David in the rubbish bin!'

It's your job to protect the baby – and to protect your older child, too, from his own anger. If he shows any signs of hurting the baby, the best rule is never to leave them alone together. When you need to go to the toilet or answer the doorbell, always take the child with you. Things were so bad for one mother that if she wanted to have a bath before the older child went to bed, she would take the baby in her crib into the bathroom and give her older child toys to play with in the corridor. She had a gate specially installed across the bathroom door so her older child could see in but not get at the baby!

It can be difficult for parents who have been looking forward so much to the arrival of their second baby to discover that their older child actually resents her a great deal. In the long run it is much easier simply to accept the fact that your child is feeling jealous and then take steps to deal with the problems as they arise. And it's worth remembering that by the end of the first year the most serious disturbances are usually over. Even the most jealous child isn't jealous all the time: there's always a mixture of emotions, including love, affection, tenderness and curiosity, as well as anger and resentment.

You child hasn't been asked if he wants a brother or sister – that's your choice and you're entitled to make it, because it's your family. So he is stuck with the consequences of your decision and has to make the best of the situation, to begin with at least. But later on he will almost certainly be grateful to you for having a sibling as a companion and playmate, even though they may quarrel as they grow older.

Try to make your older child feel as important and valuable as possible. Remember to comment on how grown up he is now and how many things he can do that the baby can't. Some young children do seem to suddenly become very independent and 'grown up' when a new baby arrives. And of course, this can be very convenient for you and makes you think your child is happy with things as they are. However, it's important to remember that this is your child's way of expressing his feelings – and this also includes some distress, resentment and rejection, as well as affection and interest in the baby, as we've already seen earlier in this chapter. So try to make sure you tell your child he doesn't always have to be grown up, as well as giving him cuddles and praise for his new skills.

The older your child is, the more responsibility you can give him in helping you look after the baby. So, for example older youngsters can mind the baby, help you bottle-feed or change a nappy and if they are strong and mature enough can hold the baby for a while, too.

However, there may be many times when he wishes he were a baby again to get all this attention and he doesn't want you to keep telling him what a big boy he is. And don't make his help with the baby the only reason he gets your approval now. Instead, make sure he is praised and appreciated for all sorts of other things that are nothing to do with the baby.

TAKING CARE OF YOUR OLDER CHILD'S NEEDS

It's very common after a new baby is born for the mother to have almost no time to play with her older child. The Cambridge survey found that many first-born children's lives changed dramatically. They got much less attention from their mother, they were more likely to be found wandering round aimlessly instead of playing with her, and not surprisingly, there were far more arguments between them.

A new baby will always take up a lot of time, and there's not much point in feeling guilty because you now have less time for your older child. However, as far as possible, try to continue to do some of the things you used to do together, so that his routine feels familiar, especially when the baby is asleep.

Tell him that you're going to have this time together and that he can choose what he wants to do with you, such as a game or a story perhaps. Something else won't get done, of course, such as the washing-up, the cooking or the cleaning, but your child's needs are more important right now.

There will be many occasions when you simply have to forgo some of his favourite activities because the baby's needs are more urgent. In such cases, it's better to acknowledge honestly the reason why you have to postpose them and to let your child know that you appreciate how he feels about this. So, for example you can say:

> It's a nuisance that I have to feed the baby now and that we can't go to the paddling pool. I know you're cross about it, but as soon as I've finished seeing to her, we'll collect everything up and go to the park.

Despite all your efforts, you may find that your older child simply does not get on with the baby. If this happens, try not to blame yourself. The surveys which have been done into how children react to each other suggest that there are several factors which are entirely outside the parents' control.

For example, the temperament of *both* children will make a difference. If your new baby takes to her older brother and responds well to him, they're likely to get on better than if the baby seems indifferent or even hostile. If your older child has a withdrawn or quiet temperament, he may find it harder to cope with a new sibling.

Some surveys suggest that two boys are likely to get on better together, or that if you have a very close relationship with your first-born daughter, she is less likely to get on with a new baby. You can't choose your children's sex or temperament, and it may be several years before your children learn to like each other. But the more you can help them express their feelings and cope with the conflict between them, the easier they'll find it to get on – not just with each other, but with other people, too, in later life.

POSTNATAL DEPRESSION

Earlier in this chapter we looked at the problem of the 'baby blues' – a mild form of depression lasting a few days or weeks at the most after the birth of a baby. But postnatal depression can be more serious, even though it only afflicts a minority of women. It's much more than the unpredictable mood swings of the early postnatal period and may include feelings of hopelessness, despair, loss of purpose and a sense of meaningless in life. The days pass without joy or colour and you feel as if there's a heavy black cloud sitting on your shoulders. There may be bouts of prolonged crying, with a sense of futility or anger with yourself and everyone around you.

In extreme and comparatively rare cases, there may be powerful destructive feelings towards yourself, such as thoughts of suicide, and aggressive feelings towards your baby or other children in the family. Some of the worst cases of child abuse arise when depression of this kind among women has been neglected or ignored.

Depression is an emotional illness and can be triggered by many major life events, including childbirth, death in the family, divorce or other kinds of loss, serious family problems or losing a job. It can occur at any time after the birth of the baby and not necessarily during the first few days, as happens with the 'baby blues'. It's common for it to crop up several months later without warning and when it happens it's a sign that you need help and shouldn't try to struggle on alone. In the most serious cases, known as *puerperal psychosis*, a stay in hospital may be necessary for some women and it's common for both mother and baby to go in together.

Medical help may include drugs to lift the depression, but practical and emotional support are just as important. For some mothers, if the depression isn't too severe, counselling may be of great help and either individual or family psychotherapy may be recommended to help the whole family work towards finding a way of coping with the problem.

Whatever the degree of depression you experience after the birth of your baby, the last thing you need to be told is to 'Pull yourself together.' And unfortunately, this is often what well-meaning people say to the mother in distress. So it's important for other people to be alert to the signs of postnatal blues and depression and to be able to get help if you're feeling too down to do it for yourself. There are many sources of support for women going through these feelings, ranging from your health visitor and doctor to a local mother and baby group where you can talk about the problems of looking after young children with others in similar situations.

In spite of feelings of depression which many women go through, there is often a mixture of elation and joy with the new-born baby. And of course, every woman experiences a sense of relief when it's all over and she finds that her baby is healthy and normal in every respect.

COPING WITH DISABILITY

So far we've been talking about coping with the normal range of problems that affect you as a mother or that occur when both children are born healthy. But there are a certain number of babies born every year with some kind of defect or disability. And in these cases, there are additional worries and stresses which parents have to cope with and which affect the way they cope with other children in the family.

Many of these defects may be relatively minor and can be corrected with surgery soon after birth or as soon as the baby is old enough. These include cleft palate problems, a dislocated hip, abnormalities of the feet, hands or limbs, or internal defects, such as problems with the heart, stomach, intestines and so on. Some babies are born with skin disorders, such as birthmarks, some of which disappear of their own accord in time, and others may need special treatment later on, or camouflage if they are more severe. And in a certain number of cases, babies are born premature and may need intensive care in a special-care baby unit for days or weeks after the birth.

Where the first child is born with a disability, parents often worry about the possibility of second or subsequent babies being born with a defect, too. This may cause them to be overanxious and very protective towards the second-born, even though she is normal and healthy. Whichever child is born unwell or with a disability, however, it often happens that they get more attention than others in the family, which can lead to feelings of exclusion and resentment by the other siblings, and results in difficult behaviour.

Whatever kind of defect a baby may have, either mental or physical, it's common for parents to have feelings of disappointment, anxiety, guilt and depression. 'Was it something I did during pregnancy that caused my baby to be born this way? Could it have been prevented?' are typical questions women ask afterwards. And of course, there's often no particular reason why a baby should be born with a disability, so no one can be blamed.

Ultimately, most parents learn to come to terms with a second child who is born 'imperfect' and learn to love him or her just as much as their first-born. It usually doesn't take very long for a parent to ignore the obvious physical handicap and to accept that their child is just as wonderful and valuable as any other, no matter what the problem. More often, the problems come from other people's attitudes, which may range from curiosity and staring to avoidance on the street for fear of not knowing what to say, inappropriate sympathy and even stupid or ignorant remarks.

This process of acceptance and coming to terms with a child's physical or mental disability can be greatly helped with proper medical advice and assistance and factual information about the condition. Parents need to have the problem adequately and sensitively explained, together with a realistic description of what will be involved in the future. This may include medical treatment to correct or stabilise the condition, or information about practical sources of help.

To assist parents in overcoming the shock of learning about a child's disability, counselling may be appropriate, to enable them to explore their complex feelings.

And for many conditions, self-help support groups exist to put parents in touch with each other, so that they don't feel so isolated and alone. Your health visitor will know of local groups or alternatively you can contact your local voluntary service council for details. See Appendix II for further details.

4 Growing up

IS SIBLING RIVALRY INEVITABLE?

Most adults who come from families with more than one child have powerful memories of their relationship with a brother or sister. Families shape our experience of the immediate world and colour the way we relate to other people for the rest of our lives. And although our most important relationship is with our parents, the hostilities and bonds we forge with siblings can also last a lifetime.

For every family with more than one child, one of the primary issues is to learn how to share – and this means sharing things people usually feel jealous and possessive about. And paradoxically, learning to handle jealousy in the context of family life does have some important advantages that are easily overlooked when we're in the thick of trying to cope with the more awful aspects of it. So, for example, two (or more) youngsters have to find a way to share their parents' love and attention, even though their dearest wish is to have that love completely undivided for themselves. They also need to learn that love isn't exclusive or finite and that if some goes to a sibling, it doesn't mean there's less for them.

This isn't an easy lesson to learn, but it's one that only children have to learn outside the family. And that's often in a much less loving or generous context, which may make it an even more painful experience for a child without siblings.

Family rivalries can help a child to grow up with a more realistic expectation of what life is like in the outside world. Learning to share and compromise are essential in the youngster who is developing from childish egocentricity into a mature awareness of the need for give and take. Becoming aware of the need to consider others is vital in successful adult relationships.

Two American psychologists, Stephen Bank and Michael Kahn, described this particular process in their book *The Sibling Bond*:

> The ability to deflect aggression, to use it wisely and at the right moment, to use humour, to surrender without debasing oneself and to defeat someone without humiliating that person, are all skills that children and adolescents can eventually use in relationships with peers, spouses and ultimately their own children.

Sharing has to be learnt at the most commonplace level of everyday life, too, whether it's learning to share a bathtub, special toys or books, a bedroom, handed-down clothing, mealtimes or television programmes. Children have to learn to share other important relationships, too. These include, for example, friendships with other children or cousins, perhaps, or with grandparents, favourite uncles and aunts or with a special neighbourhood friend.

And then there are the ups and downs of family life which make up the fabric of our childhood and adolescent experience, which all children in the home share, regardless, simply because they live together under one roof. Celebrations like Easter, Passover, Christmas, Ramadan, New Year, Diwali, birthdays, holidays and other special happy events all help to create a fund of pleasant memories about being together and sharing in fun, laughter and festive meals.

There are also the more painful experiences that none of us can escape and affect all families at some time or another. Illness, death of a beloved relative, loss of a pet, the absence of a parent for some reason, divorce and a host of other mildly or severely traumatic events are also experiences that youngsters share. And these can create a bond for the rest of their lives that's special, simply because they shared it at such a formative stage when they may have also leaned on each other for hope, encouragement, and support in their grief. Here's how Alison, mother of three, puts it:

> I feel I know when the chips are down, they are together. They face life together. Inside that circle there's a lot of struggle, competition, jealousy, difficulty, but for the outside world they've got each other.

But the fact remains, that although we may choose our friendships and our marriage partners, we are not able to choose our brothers and sisters. Friends and spouses can be (and often are) changed – but we're stuck with the brothers and sisters in our family and can't do anything about them until we're old enough to leave home. So for many youngsters, it's a matter of enduring a relationship with a sibling they may not be able to stand much of the time, until the passing years and maturity make things easier to handle. Here's a long-term view in the words of Sally:

> What happens now doesn't say anything about the relationship in later life – and that is longer and more important and more lasting than a few years in childhood. When my sister went away to school, I wrote to her every day. When another sister went to university, I still used to see her every week. Now that we've got children of our own, we're just as close.

For other parents, the hostilities may be relatively minor and two or more youngsters may seem, to outsiders at least, to be in a rather close and loving relationship. Alison describes how other children appear to her – but not her own!

> I used to look at people whose children loved each other – my sister has four children and they love each other. There's a photo of them with their arms wound round each other... One of my friends comes home and finds her three children entwined together in one bed! And I see friends' kids embrace each other in the playground and kiss each other as one goes off somewhere.

Learning how to share and competing for time, love, attention and possession are a fact of life for every sibling. For some, this learning can be relatively painless, while for others it can last, alas, until the children are old enough to leave home.

It's we parents who, when driven to distraction by the regular fights or bickering that so many children seem to engage in (and usually enjoy!), often wonder why we ever imagined that family life would be happier with two children rather than one. Coping with the endless round of quarrels can try the patience of the most saintly parent – and most of us have rather shorter fuses that can lead to blow-ups much more frequently than we ever thought ourselves capable of.

For many of us, the decision to have a second child is influenced by the powerful and widespread ideas that an only child may be spoilt and that two offspring will be friends and companions for each other all their lives. What we often don't bargain for are the strong feelings of jealousy, rage and anger that crop up in the first-born child that we've already looked at in Chapter 3. And when the competition and jealousy persist for years between the siblings, even the most dedicated and loving parent can become worn down with the effort of trying to maintain harmony in the home between the warring youngsters.

Sometimes, of course, there can be a sudden and unexpected shift in the relationship between siblings that fight. The arrival of a third (or fourth) child, can lead to unity in the face of another rival.

A few parents do, however, seem to sail unscathed through family life with several children who squabble and fight for most of the childhood and teenage years. They are temperamentally suited to parenting a large family, often because they are able to remain calm and not too caught up in their children's battles.

Although sibling rivalry is virtually a foregone conclusion when you have more than one child, the extent to which it is a problem varies considerably from one family to another. Sometimes this may be due to the way in which the parents handle the jealousy when it occurs, and sometimes it's because the children themselves may have temperaments which are more or less disposed towards jealousy.

For children to develop their inner strength and resources, the normal family conflicts and jealousy have to be handled constructively and creatively by the parents concerned. This means that you and your partner need to be aware of not damaging a child's self-esteem, even when she behaves in ways that are unacceptable. To destroy a child's confidence and belief in herself is the fastest way to create insecurity, anxiety and jealousy of others.

Competition and rivalry are fostered by feelings of insecurity and the possible withdrawal of love or attention, and they are diminished when a child knows she is secure and that the love won't disappear when she does something that's not acceptable. When a child feels basically accepted and trusted for who she is, she begins to let go of jealous feelings. Like feelings of inadequacy and worthlessness, jealousy only thrives when we think the other person is going to 'do us down', that we will lose out in some way if we don't 'fight for our share of the cake', or that we will be despised because the other person is somehow 'better than us'.

The youngster who grows up believing that she is lovable and worthy in her own right will be the one who is able to respect herself. Respecting oneself means it becomes possible to respect other people without feeling threatened by them.

DOES 'EQUAL' MEAN 'THE SAME'?

One of the most important factors in helping children to develop a good sense of self-esteem is to treat each one as a unique individual in their own right, with their own temperament, personality, talents and needs.

Most caring parents wants to be fair to their children and for many people being *fair* means treating children *identically*. But treating children identically means that we have to ignore their differences and their uniqueness. So, for example, if Mary aged six has 50 pence pocket money each week, then it's 'fair' that Danny aged eight gets the same amount. Or if Tommy gets a new pair of boots because his old ones are worn out, then Billy also has to have a new item of clothing to stop him feeling jealous, regardless of whether he needs it or not.

The intention behind this attitude is positive because it's meant to prevent the feeling of favouritism among children and to convey the idea that the children in the family are equally loved. And there's no doubt that for one child to be favoured over another is a certain recipe for jealous feelings. But treating children identically is *not* the best way to counter this problem.

The way parents can foster a sense of being uniquely valued in each child is to make each relationship a *special* one. Each child needs to be treated separately – not loved more or less than another but in their own special way – for *who* they are and not for *what* they do or *how* they behave.

There are families where the differences between children are very great. Examples of this include talent in a particular child while the others are of average ability, or outstanding beauty in another child, or physical illness or disability or mental handicap and so on. In cases of this kind it's possible to argue that one child will naturally get more attention than the others, which can lead to difficult relationships between the other children and the parents.

An example of a disabled sibling is given by Stephen Bank and Michael Kahn in their book, *The Sibling Bond*. In this particular case, a mother had one seriously handicapped older son, Adam, and a younger son, Mark, who was healthy. The mother gave Adam a great deal of attention, found him specialised treatment and helped him to develop his abilities to a remarkable degree. Mark was clingy and dependent and had a tendency to exaggerate any minor injury or complaint into a major problem.

The psychologist who worked with the family discovered that the mother had always tried to prevent Mark from outshining Adam and had unconsciously held him back. And Mark had had to 'invent' his own ailments in order to attract the love and attention his mother lavished on his brother.

In cases of this kind it's even more vital for parents to treat each child as a unique person and give them what they need in order to develop their full potential. If Mark had had his rightful share of attention, he would not have needed to develop his hypochondria. Treating both children as individuals with special needs and without comparing them would have enabled them to develop in their own way and would have allowed them to enjoy each other's successes, no matter how great or small they were.

'EQUAL' PUNISHMENT

It's tempting for parents sometimes to blame or punish both children when there's a misdemeanour and the faults can't be easily appointed. So when youngsters fight and a vase is broken, Dad may simply blame both of them because it's easier and mete out the same punishment regardless of how the accident happened. This is also a common tactic in the classroom. Most adults remember being punished by a teacher because of a fellow classmate's misbehaviour – and the angry feelings that went with the sense of injustice. The basic message behind this approach is: 'If she's bad, you're bad, too. There's no difference between you.'

'WHO DO YOU LOVE BEST, MUMMY?'

It's common for young children to ask the question: 'Who do you love most, Mummy – Barbara or me?' in order to find out who is the favourite of the moment. This is a searching question, designed to test the idea that your love can only be divided up like a cake and to establish a pecking order in the family hierarchy. And such a question can take us by surprise when we realise that perhaps we may favour one child over another, because they're easier to get on with or because they're more like ourselves in certain ways.

If your child asks you this question, it's important not to fall into the trap of giving the impression that you favour one child over another. Say something like: 'I love you both – you're both very special to me. You and Barbara are very different in lots of ways and I love you both for who you are.'

This kind of response communicates that you appreciate their individuality and their lovability for themselves, without comparing them either favourably or unfavourably with each other.

You can help your child to understand the idea of loving more than one person at a time by asking her in turn about her love for you and your partner. When she realises that she loves both her Mummy and Daddy because they are who they are and that loving one doesn't mean she can't love the other, then your child will also begin to appreciate the way you love her and her sibling.

It's rare, in fact, for a parent to be completely even-handed in their affection and love for all of their children, regardless of how much of an ideal this may be. Some parents find infancy a trying time in a child's life, while others find the adolescent years the toughest to deal with. The love and strength of the relationship may be severely tested during the difficult stages of a child's growing years and there are many parents who hesitate to admit that there are times in a child's life when they may actually dislike their offspring.

On top of this, it often happens that one child may be going through a difficult stage when the other one isn't – and it can become very easy to reinforce the problems with the difficult one. Your second baby at around fifteen or eighteen months may be at a delightful stage of starting to walk and talk, yet still very cuddly with some growing independence but not having temper tantrums yet.

Your three- or four-year-old, however, may not be so easy. She's veering between aggressive independence and whiny neediness, resenting the attention you give to the baby, making it very difficult for you to feel you love them 'equally'.

> Richard's eighteen months old now – and gorgeous. He's very charming, a real little flirt and everyone he meets comments on it! He's happy almost all of the time, full of laughter, mischievous but a joy to be with. There are days when I seem to have nothing but fights with Sally. She's three and sometimes I can't do anything right with her. I suddenly thought that when *she* was eighteen months, her life had been turned upside-down with the arrival of a new baby. She always saw me holding him and got far fewer cuddles of her own. And now he's eighteen months, and I'm still cuddling him.

WHAT IF YOU DISLIKE YOUR CHILD?

It sometimes happens that a parent finds she dislikes one of her children. There may be something about the child's appearance, physique or personality that just seems to be a constant irritation. In some families, these feelings may be quite open and the parent may tell the child and everyone knows exactly what is happening.

In other families, however, the parent may be so ashamed or worried about her feelings that she does her best to cover them up. Molly, whose two daughters are now grown up, found herself in this situation:

> Of course, I loved both my children. But I always knew that if they hadn't been my children or if they'd just been people I happened to meet, I'd have chosen Veronica (my eldest) as a *friend*, and not Susan.

So I always felt I had to make it up to Susan by being particularly careful with her, doing the things she liked. And even today, Veronica is still angry with me because she felt left out a lot of the time and felt that Susan was the favourite – even though she knows that it was really the other way round.

Disliking one child strongly, or feeling constantly irritated with her, can be a sign that feelings from your past are getting in the way of your relationship with her. You may find it helpful to ask yourself a few questions:

- Who does this child remind me of?
- Who does she look like?
- Is she like my side of the family, or her father's?

Family therapists ask people about their family 'trees' in order to find out what family patterns may be at work when the relationships are troubled. They often find that a parent who dislikes or stereotypes a child is actually identifying the child with someone from their own childhood about whom they felt very strongly. One couple we spoke to explained the problems they had when their second child was born:

> We'd been so happy with our first baby. But our second was hard to feed and just wouldn't settle to the breast or bottle. He always seemed to be crying for more. We went and saw a therapist who had helped us some years earlier and ended up talking about our own siblings. Both of us are first children, and we each have unhappy relationships with our second siblings who are both unemployed and have a drink problem. The therapist suggested that we were identifying our new baby with our younger siblings, who were also – as he put it – dirty, greedy and always at the bottle! We were terribly shocked at the idea, but we began to realise that feeling bad about our two siblings had stopped us feeling good about our second son. Now we adore him just as much.

A parent who is really irritated by a particular characteristic in her partner may see the same one in their child. In one family we know, the mother, whose own marriage was unsatisfactory, found it very hard to get on with her second daughter. She always insisted that this daughter looked 'just like her father' (making it clear that this was nothing to be proud of!). In fact, family photographs showed that the second daughter looked very like her mother as a young girl. Not until the girls had grown up did the mother become close to her second daughter and appreciate her many talents.

Family patterns of this kind can be very damaging. But they can be changed. Confronting problems from your own childhood can help sort out how you truly feel about your child and make it easier to see her as she really is. Just talking about the situation with your partner or a friend can help a great deal. But if you still find yourself rejecting one child, you can get help from a family therapist or counsellor. (See page 119 for sources of help.)

COMPARISONS BREED JEALOUSY

One of the most effective – and devastating – ways that parents unwittingly foster jealousy between siblings is to compare them with each other. Examples of this kind of comparison are: 'Your sister does her sums much faster than you', or 'You're such a messy child – your brother was much tidier than you.'

Comments like this pave the way to resentment because their effect is to make the child feel inadequate. It is baffling why so many adults consistently use this as a method to get children to change when it's so obviously counter-productive and just achieves the opposite of the intended effect. The main reason why it's such a common tactic among adults is because they're so used to being compared from their own childhood, that it is almost automatic to do it with their own children.

Next time you catch yourself thinking or talking in comparisons about your own children, try imagining how you would feel in a similar situation. Suppose your partner says over dinner one evening after you've spent hours preparing something special: 'Why don't you cook as well as my mother? Her food is so delicious and the table always looks so pretty.'

It wouldn't be surprising if you felt furious about being made to feel hopeless as a cook compared with your mother-in-law. You would understandably feel hurt and angry at your partner's insensitivity, and quite probably jealous of your mother-in-law being held up as a model cook. And if you were repeatedly unfavourably compared with her, there might come a time when you would be delighted to put her in a bad light to get your revenge. Eventually, after hearing remarks about your bad cooking often enough, you'd probably give it up altogether, having decided that it was no longer worth the effort, as you were definitely no good at it.

Being unfavourably compared with a sibling can also lead to an unexpected and unintended effect. For example, a child who is constantly being told that her older sister is cleverer or more beautiful or more artistic (or whatever else the parents value) is likely not only to be jealous, but also to adopt the attitude that she can never compete by being good at these things, so she might as well do her best to be bad at them! Extreme 'naughtiness' and other difficult behaviour can often be traced back to a time where a child has given up the attempt to win attention through a parent's approval and has instead decided to be the 'best at being bad' as a way of getting attention.

You certainly don't feel grateful to anyone who undermines your self-esteem and confidence. On the contrary, we all – adults and children alike – need words of genuine encouragement and appreciation from people we care about. We don't need destructive comparisons that can so easily chip away at a hard-won sense of identity and individuality. And interestingly enough, they're also damaging to the child who benefits by the comparisons, because they tend to generate a sense of smugness and superiority which in turn only aggravates the jealous feelings.

So the temptation to make comparisons is virtually automatic and it can take a real and conscious effort of will to avoid doing it. However, one of the best ways of overcoming this tendency to make comparisons between our children is to avoid using *value judgements* about them as much as possible.

If there is something your child does or doesn't do that you dislike, it's much more effective to *describe* the behaviour directly, rather than to comment on what another child does by way of comparison. So, instead of saying, for example: 'Your sister does her sums much faster than you', you might say instead: 'I can see you're really trying hard with those sums.' In this way you leave out the irrelevant reference to her sister and simply comment on what you see your child doing, with no implication that she's better or worse at it.

Children are very adept anyway at comparing themselves with their siblings and friends, and don't need encouragement from adults. Keeping in mind the importance of valuing and loving each child for their uniqueness, rather than for how they compare with a sibling, is a very useful way to break the habit of making comparisons.

HOW LABELS AFFECT CHILDREN

Another devilish trick many adults unwittingly use to breed rivalry is to stereotype their children by attaching labels to them. Typical of this are remarks like these: 'Oh, our Stella has always been the brainy one in the family', 'Johnny's the sporting one.'

This kind of pigeonholing is endless and familiar to most of us. Labels like 'bossy', 'stupid', 'messy', 'artistic', 'clever', 'pretty', 'adventurous', 'naughty', 'good', 'bad' and so on may be convenient when describing a child but have the negative effect of encouraging children to live up to those labels, both good and bad, and to limit the other possible ways of seeing and valuing themselves.

So, for example, a child labelled as 'brainy' may believe that to win approval, she must always excel at school and in exams and that if she doesn't she's a failure. Her sibling may grow up feeling she can't be brainy because she doesn't have this label and there's only room for one brainy child in the family anyway (that's what labels are for, after all). So she gives up every effort to do well at school and perhaps concentrates on living up to her particular label, which may be 'beautiful'.

Or, on the other hand, the 'beautiful' child may be jealous of the 'brainy' one, because in that family being clever is more highly valued than being attractive. Being 'beautiful' is a second-rate attribute disguised as a compliment – a powerful message which the child absorbs unconsciously. The two children then become stereotyped falsely in ways which can seriously limit their future development, if the conditioning is very strong – which it often is.

Here's how Mary describes her battle against labelling with her five sons:

> They're terribly different people ... Being of the same sex has a big effect. I do call them all 'the boys'. I don't worry about lumping them all together, but I do worry about labelling the children. You read that later on, children really resent having been labelled 'the clever one' or the 'pretty one', or the 'sweet one' or whatever, and that's exactly what we've done with the children ...

Labels are another example of value judgements that, like comparisons, we often make about our children without really thinking about the consequences.

And they often influence our own attitudes, even though we may be unaware of this. For example, a child who is called 'musical' may be the only one in the family who is encouraged to take piano lessons, because she has the gift. The other children may miss out on a musical education, because they're thought to be no good at it, even though they might have had enormous pleasure from it.

On the other hand, the parents may decide that to be 'fair', *all* the children have to have music lessons to avoid favouritism, even though only one wants them. Both attitudes are mistaken, since the better way is to give each child lessons or opportunities which are suited to his or her needs, talents and wishes, without comparing them with each other at all. So that might mean football for one child, ballet for another, gymnastics for a third and computers for another.

Once we become aware of what we're doing, it becomes easier to avoid falling into the pattern of labelling children. The use of description to praise children (and adults, too!) is more powerful and effective in communicating our interest and support than a value judgement.

So, instead of perhaps saying to your child: 'That's a lovely present you've made for me. You really are such a clever little girl!' – vague, unspecific praise that suggests your child only gets approval when you think she's clever – an alternative might be to say: 'I feel so happy with the gift you've given me. And I really like the way you wrapped it up so neatly with that pretty red and blue paper and red and white striped ribbon with this white bow on top.' – specific praise that lets the child know how you feel about her gift and that you've noticed how much trouble she's taken and her skill in wrapping it.

The same approach is useful when you want to avoid using negative labels about your children, too. It's easy, when we're upset or angry, to tell a child that she's 'bad' or 'naughty' when she does something we don't like. But with the descriptive approach, your comment could be something like this: 'When you punch Johnnie, it hurts him and I get upset and cross. It's not allowed to hit your brother.'

This kind of comment lets your child know that the behaviour is unacceptable but also that she's not a bad person because she behaves like this. Once she believes she's bad, it will be hard for her to believe that she is a good person. But if you tell her that she's doing something that's unacceptable, at least, she can change that. If she's a bad person, she can't change her badness, but she can change her behaviour.

So avoiding labelling and making comparisons between youngsters are two ways of helping to prevent friction and jealousy between them. It needs to be remembered that sibling rivalry is virtually inevitable in every family, unless the children are very widely spaced. And while its impact may vary according to the temperaments of your offspring, the best you can hope for is to prevent unnecessary competition and to moderate what you can't prevent.

Conflict and rivalry are a part of growing up in a family and their absence suggests that there is probably something amiss in the relationship between parents and children, just as an excess of them would also indicate that all wasn't well. Dorothy Corkille Briggs is an American family counsellor and parent educator of many years experience, as well as author of *Your Child's Self-Esteem*. In her view a relaxed, cooperative and democratic home life are some of the essential building blocks for a harmonious and happy family.

An ability to give and take, to share freely with each other and a sense of freedom and independence outside the home are among the gifts that parents can give to their children, both in their words and in their behaviour. Where children feel special and valued for themselves and loved uniquely by their parents, they are more likely to be able to share with each other without feeling threatened by their siblings.

SCHOOLS AND SIBLINGS

Most parents assume that children will follow each other to the same school. Many schools encourage this by giving priority to younger siblings of a child already at the school. But it's not always the best policy. Some teachers make very damaging comparisons between an older child who's excelled at sport or exams, for example, and a younger child who's not so gifted.

Molly took a different view:

> When I was young, we all went to different schools – my parents wouldn't have dreamt of sending us to the same one. With my three children, I tried to find the school that would suit each of them best. Two of them did go to the same primary, but my youngest loved music and I wanted a school that would give her lots of opportunities to play instruments and sing.

Even if you do end up with the same school for your children, perhaps because there's not much choice locally, considering which school would suit each one best is another useful way of thinking about their individual needs.

THE MIDDLE PATH

Many parents are confused about the kind of relationship they want to have with their children. For some, who have been brought up strictly by their own parents, with perhaps a distant, uninvolved and rather authoritarian father, the idea of repeating this with their own children seems unacceptable.

Such parents can sometimes swing to the opposite extreme and adopt a *laissez-faire* attitude towards their children, with minimal interference in what they do or say. This kind of upbringing can produce children who are wild and uncontrollable, thoughtless and rude and who have little respect for other people or their belongings.

Other parents believe in authority and discipline and find using physical punishment acceptable in bringing up young children. Some justify it on the grounds that, 'It never did me any harm to be spanked when I was young.' There is plenty of evidence that this harsh approach of strict discipline and rigid patterns of upbringing certainly can produce children who are well-behaved and obedient. But they are not usually very happy and their obedience is usually based on fear of punishment, rather than from self-discipline.

Recent research by John and Elizabeth Newson of Nottingham University Child Development Research Unit has shown that there is 'a very clear association' between the physical punishment of children at the age of eleven and their delinquent behaviour (such as stealing, truancy and troublesomeness at school, with the neighbours and with police). They conclude that:

> What we can say is smacking and beating mothers do not succeed in producing non-delinquent children, and the dictum of 'spare the rod and spoil the child' can't be upheld by these findings.

Most parents fall somewhere in between the two extremes of using strict, punitive methods based on the idea that the parent's needs are all-important and very permissive ones based on the idea that the children's needs are all-important. The recent attention which has been focused on the effects of physical abuse and corporal punishment on children is making more and more people begin to question smacking as a means of discipline, even as a last resort.

Apart from anything else, many parents realise that if they don't want their children to hit each other as a way of resolving conflict or expressing strong feelings, than it's important that they shouldn't use hitting themselves as a method of discipline. It's hardly fair to blame your children for being physically violent to each other when you yourself are using violence towards them.

One mother we talked to was shocked to find herself slapping one of her children unthinkingly:

> Sally suddenly shoved her brother hard enough to push him over. I was tired and slapped her on the backside and said: 'Don't you dare hit your brother!' The minute I did it, I realised how stupid it was – so I apologised to Sally and said nobody was allowed to hit – ever.

The strategies and ideas suggested in this book are based on what can be loosely called a 'middle path' between the two extremes and rests on the assumption that the needs of both parents and children are *equally* important. Of course, there are times when the needs of one or the other may have to take precedence because of some kind of urgency in a situation, but otherwise, the art of successful family living lies in balancing all the different sets of needs justly and democratically.

The way you communicate this message to your children will be implied in the quality of your relationship with them, the kind of language you use when you talk to them and the nonverbal messages (such as smiling, your expressions and other kinds of body language). Sometimes, of course, you need to point things out to your youngsters more explicitly when they complain (as they're bound to, at some time) that you're not being fair.

So when your older child gets jealous of a younger sibling, you can try pointing out the privileges that age brings and then ask if she would like to switch roles. If the offer is accepted, your older one is treated just the same as the younger, including going to bed earlier, having less pocket money or watching less television and so on. This kind of experiment soon gets the message about individual needs across!

As we develop as parents with the experience of each successive child, it becomes clear as to how we might have done things differently if we'd only known the pitfalls in advance. In particular there are certain guidelines that may be useful to keep in mind when handling the children as they arrive.

THE POSITION IN THE FAMILY

The position of children in the family is an important factor in influencing rivalry, although this is only a tendency, rather than a constant pattern. So, for example, it's common for the first-born to be jealous of the new baby and for this jealousy to last for months or even years, as we've already seen in the previous chapter. The second-born child may also be jealous of the subsequent one, and this can go on down through the family, although possibly weakening because of the presence of older children who ensure that mother's attention is less devoted to a single child anyway. A second-born can also be jealous of the *first* and want more attention herself.

First-born children tend to be the ones who get the most time and attention simply because they're the only one present to start with. They're also the ones we make our mistakes with and worry about most. Parents tend to be stricter with first-borns and expect more from them in terms of behaviour and performance at school and so on. So it's worth trying to make sure that you aren't too demanding with your eldest child, that your standards aren't unreasonably high and that you have realistic expectations of your youngster's stages of development.

It's wise to avoid being authoritarian with this child particularly, as first-borns tend to be bossy and domineering with their younger siblings. They're also more perfectionist on the whole than later children, so avoid being too critical in order to discourage this characteristic.

There is a risk with first-born children – and girls in particular – that they end up 'mothering' the younger children. Often this is seen as being beneficial for the eldest, because it gives her experience of coping with younger ones and there is some truth in this. On the other hand, it's important to remember that the baby needs *adult* attention, love and teaching, and not a sibling substitute. It's also worth remembering that the first-born may be suppressing her own needs in order to cope with a younger sibling.

It's easy for parents to regard the older girl as 'mature' or 'independent' or 'being good' when she takes care of a baby, especially because it's such a welcome relief for an overworked mother! Your first-born may well become very resentful or angry at the unfair burden placed on her by such expectations and your baby risks being denied real mothering by you.

Your second-born child may also be jealous of the eldest, and particularly of the privileges that being older often brings. Going to bed later, getting more pocket money, watching 'grown-up' television programmes and films, and being allowed greater independence outside the home are typical issues that fuel jealousy towards an older sibling. And this kind of jealousy often lasts well into the teenage years with bitter quarrels and fighting all the way.

Second-born children also have advantages and disadvantages in their position in the family. They may not get as much attention as the older child did from you, but they do benefit from the attention of the older child, who often acts as a 'teacher' as we've already seen. Sometimes second-borns can reach their milestones of development faster, as Mandy reports:

> My younger daughter gave up breastfeeding earlier than my older one had. It wasn't because there were any problems, but she saw her sister eating with us at the table and wanted to copy her. It was the same with talking. Her sister talked to her a great deal so she heard more language round her and started to use it early on. And she began to walk sooner, because she could keep up with her sister in that way, too.

Sometimes, however, the opposite may happen and a younger sibling's development may be slowed down. This need not be because of any inherent problem, but because the older one tends to do things for them which means they have less incentive to talk or crawl.

If this happens with your children, you can suggest that your older child becomes a 'teacher', rather than a 'doer' for the younger one. Use encouraging sentences like:

> Now show Billy how to stack the bricks and then how to make them fall down. Then ask him to stack them up again.

or:

> Why don't you read this picture book to Billy and ask him to show you all the different kinds of animals.

With your middle child, remember that it can be uncomfortable being squashed between the oldest and the youngest (if you have three children). The middle one can often feel lost and neglected, so it's sensible to make sure you single this one out for special attention and ensure that she gets time with you on her own.

The middle child needs the opportunity to develop her own identity as a separate person from her older and younger siblings, who will inevitably have had more attention than her. Being in the middle often means having to bend and adapt to the needs of siblings, so it's important to be alert to this possibility.

The youngest child is frequently referred to as 'the baby of the family' even when she is old and grey! This kind of label is more than just a joke – it's often a reality for many last-born children who may have been indulged more than the others, been expected to assume fewer responsibilities and probably had a more relaxed and easy-going upbringing than the older siblings.

To compensate for this tendency, it's wise to encourage your last-born to be as responsible as your older children (but don't overdo it, of course), to avoid the 'baby' label as much as possible so that she doesn't feel she has to live up to it and to discourage the attitudes of indulgence among relatives and family friends.

Older siblings often tease or torment the youngest, partly as a way of taking revenge for their own hurt or sense of injustice on someone smaller than themselves. Sometimes this teasing is good-natured and the effect is to treat the last-born as a kind of toy or pet, rather than a real person. And in return, youngest children may find the best way to get back at this behaviour is to become manipulative or whining. So prevent your older children from this kind of destructive behaviour and encourage your last-born to be direct and open in expressing her complaints and needs.

SEX AND FAVOURITISM

Children of the same sex may compare themselves favourably or unfavourably with each other and compete for looks, clothing, girl or boyfriends, possessions, money and parental favours. With children of different sexes, some of this competition doesn't arise, such as over clothes, appearance or boy or girlfriends. But jealousy can and often does arise when children think they're being unfairly treated with regard to household chores, for example, which often get divided up according to the child's sex.

It's common in many families for the girls to be expected to cook, clean, wash up, sew, iron and undertake most of the tasks that her mother regards as a woman's role. And for boys it's expected that they will follow in their father's footsteps and either do no housework at all or only those jobs regarded as the 'proper' work of men, such as mending fuses, DIY tasks, gardening, bicycle and car repairs and so on.

And although many couples regard themselves as much more egalitarian in their roles than their parents were, they often fall into the traditional stereotyped male and female roles once the first baby arrives. This is partly because the ideas most of us absorb at a very early age about how men and women behave by observing our own parents tend to surface again once we become parents. But another equally important aspect is the simple fact that most women stay at home to look after their babies and young children, while their partners go out to earn the money to maintain the family.

Even the most 'liberated' of couples find it difficult to avoid repeating their parents' pattern of the woman waiting on the man. And this pattern is still frequently passed on to the children, even when both parents are working in full-time jobs. The result of this different treatment of boys and girls in the same family is that by the time they reach their teenage years there may be a lot of stored-up resentment about the fact that girls on the whole are expected to work harder in the home than boys are.

'My brother was always the favoured one. He got off so lightly when it came to household chores' is a complaint commonly heard by counsellors and psychotherapists when they begin to explore the tricky area of sibling jealousy in their client's emotional history.

If you add to this the greater freedom and independence that most teenage boys have compared with their sisters, then it's not hard to see why girls often feel they get a raw deal. In the past, when there was a much greater acceptance of the division of work according to sex, there probably wasn't this kind of jealousy or resentment. So it's a fairly recent phenomenon that has accompanied the newer thinking about equality between men and women and the fairer sharing of work both in and out of the home.

Many women find it extremely difficult to break out of old patterns, however, no matter how much they find the idea of equality attractive and completely reasonable. Here's how one woman describes the problem as she experienced it:

> My mother waited hand and foot on my father, and never questioned this attitude. She did the same to my two brothers, while I was expected to be like her in the home and run round making the beds, doing the ironing for them and so on. I used to feel so angry with them, and with her and vowed I wouldn't do that with my children. But sure enough, when my husband gets home worn out after work, there I am, getting him everything he needs, no matter how tired I am, too. I'm just like my mother, putting myself and my needs last... It's such a battle to avoid setting up a stereotype for my own little girl's behaviour and attitudes.

Many women will echo this mother's words as they recognise the problems that lie in overcoming the stereotyping of hundreds of years. Ultimately, it requires the conscious effort and goodwill of both partners to lay the foundation of a more cooperative relationship and equal sharing in the home. When small children see their parents consulting, discussing and taking turns doing household chores, they have a strong model on which to base their own future relationships.

DEALING WITH CONFLICT

How you handle conflict between your children will have a big effect on the whole family. Some parents are afraid of conflict, often because their own parents avoided expressing anger in their childhood. In such cases, they find it very hard to deal with – not just between their children, but also with their partner or at work.

If you find it hard to cope with anger, you may risk becoming your children's 'referee' by continually stepping in to sort out a disagreement, perhaps before it's become serious. This may make you feel like a loving and concerned parent, but you're also preventing your children from learning how to deal with their own anger and conflict.

You may overreact in other ways, too, by becoming very upset if your children fight, for example, by screaming at them, or bursting into tears and so on. If your children learn that you consistently react to their conflict in this way, they will get the message that disagreements are something to be afraid of. They may discover ways to fight with each other in secret, rather than run the risk of upsetting you with their quarrels. Or, more likely, they will start to suppress their disagreements and anger with each other so that they get driven underground, rather than being dealt with openly.

In this way they never learn how to handle the conflicts that will inevitably arise in their personal relationships in later life. And so the pattern of avoiding anger and conflict becomes 'imprinted' on the next generation.

Some parents adopt a strategy of giving in to the older or more aggressive child's demands when there is a quarrel, while others simply take no notice in the hope that it will go away. Both of these are passive ways of handling conflict, however, and neither are effective methods of teaching children how to resolve their differences.

There is a fine line between too much interference in your children's quarrels and failing to protect a child who needs help. If one child is constantly picked on, or teased or beaten, then she needs your protection. Some parents persuade themselves that one child is 'just kidding' when another is suffering real humiliation, or that spitefulness is 'just teasing', or that physical abuse is only a 'bit of larking around'.

In such cases, failing to intervene can damage a child seriously. One man who knew that we were writing this book – a successful, professional man in his fifties – spoke bitterly about his parents' failure to protect him from his three older brothers. For years, they ganged up on him, sneered at him for being 'stupid', nicknamed him 'dummy', and ensured that he grew up feeling inferior and inadequate.

TIPS ON STAYING SANE

There are days in every parent's life when things just don't go right at home. You're on edge, busy with too many things to think about, the children are squabbling, the phone never stops ringing and then the rowing starts to escalate. Things are beginning to really get out of hand and you're in no mood to deal rationally with the fighting. Instead you finish up screaming and shouting at them, possibly hitting them, which you swore you'd never do, and then everyone collapses in tears. And to make matters worse, you feel angry and ashamed of yourself for losing control and for not behaving like the ideal mother you always saw yourself as.

Because of the pressures of life, it's often more convenient to treat all the youngsters in the same way and at the same time with general routines such as washing, dressing and telling stories. But fights often happen as a result and it can be better to solve this diffferently, as Alison discovered:

> So you look at the stress points in your day and you change them. I always used to bath my three together and there would always be a row. Now they have separate baths. You give one a bath in the morning, one in the evening, whatever works. Try a change and give them a new routine. We used to sit on the bed with me trying to read the same bedtime book together and them fighting over it. I should have said: 'Dick, you go upstairs and look at a book.' Now I put Lucy in her cot and she can see me reading to Tom, and then I read to Lucy.

So to help you save your sanity on days like these, here are some tips on coping with unruly youngsters and defusing tricky situations before tempers really rise:

- If the children are quarrelling over a toy, game or some other object and find themselves unable to agree or share, remove the object of their attention for a reasonable period of time. Offer alternative activities, explaining why you've taken this line and that they can have the original one back when they can agree to share it properly or take turns.
- Children often fight when something has to be shared between them – a piece of cake or a bowl of strawberries, for example. A useful tip is to say that one child can divide it up into portions and the other can choose her piece first!
- Use your kitchen timer to set a fixed period of time (which you decide on) when the children have to remain still and calm. The length of time is determined by your need for peace and quiet and the intensity of the fighting! Tell them they can resume their activities after the timer has rung, as long as there's no more fighting. Reimpose the silence if it starts again or use a stronger measure.
- If rules are abused (and household rules should be kept to a minimum anyway), then give adequate warning about your state of mind ('I'm beginning to feel angry/irritated/impatient . . .' and so on) and then suspend a relevant privilege if the rowing continues. This could be something like not watching a particular television programme, or missing a treat of some kind.
- If the children are arguing over taking turns, a useful way of making the decision is to choose a number yourself between, say, zero and ten and write it down on a piece of paper out of sight. Then ask them each to choose a number and the one who gets the nearest to yours gets first turn, the next nearest second turn and so on.
- It's very useful for youngsters to be able to channel their angry feelings in a harmless way. Older children can find it useful to keep a

notebook to write down their resentments and complaints about their siblings every time they get upset. Or they can do a drawing to show how angry they feel, or make plasticine or clay models of their siblings and themselves.
- Another way to help them let off steam safely is for you to give them physical activities. Punching an old pillow or cushion instead of a sibling is one idea, or you can get an angry child to kick a football round the garden.
- Encourage your children to use words to express their feelings towards each other, rather than their fists. Say something like: 'It's not allowed to punch each other, no matter how angry you are. Tell each other in words how you feel!'
- As soon as they are old enough to understand, begin to teach them how to make agreements and 'contracts' with each other which are binding and fair to everyone. You need to act as a kind of referee to give each one a fair chance to speak and express their feelings fully. With older children, you can write on a large sheet of paper what has been agreed, ask each one to sign it and post it somewhere prominently. Agree amongst you on trying it out for, say, a week or two and then see if you need to make any changes. This approach may sound very formal and businesslike but many families find it a useful process of decision-making over difficult issues and develop their own modifications according to their needs.

  Here's how it might work. Suppose your children are quarrelling over television programmes and you want to reach a sensible agreement between them. After discussion and listening to everyone's point of view, the agreement might read as follows:

  > Goal: To find a fair way for Timmy and Terry to watch their favourite TV programmes:
  > Rule One: We agree that Timmy can watch his programmes on Wednesday, Thursday and Friday.
  > Rule Two: Terry can watch his on Monday, Tuesday and Saturday.
  > Rule Three: We will try this for two weeks and see if we want to change it then.
  >
  > Signed: Timmy and Terry   Date: 10 November

- Getting children together to discuss areas of disagreement can be done using a 'family conference' style of approach. Some families set aside a particular time each week to explore problems and to agree on rules or behaviour, or to discuss plans for family activities. This is a valuable way to make everyone feel involved in decision-making and means there's less likelihood of sabotage from one of the children.

- If children are noisy or boisterous and you want to restore some order so everyone gets a chance to be heard, try using the 'talking stick' approach (based on an idea adapted from native American Indians). An object, such as a special piece of carved wood, a large shell such as a conch, or anything similar can be used to symbolise the right to speak and be listened to. At discussion times, the stick (or shell and so on) is held by one person at a time and no one is allowed to interrupt or speak unless the object is passed on to him or her. This guarantees a fair hearing for everyone.
- Sometimes a child becomes physically or verbally aggressive in a quarrel, in which case you need to think carefully about how to deal with the situation. It's unwise to reward an aggressive child with lots of attention because this will tend to reinforce the likelihood of its happening again. Even yelling or shouting at her is a kind of reward and is often better than no attention at all. So give your attention to the victim first and try to ignore the aggressive child as a way of making it clear that aggression doesn't pay.
- In some situations, a child becomes so physically aggressive towards another that it's necessary for you to intervene. Hold the aggressor firmly from behind in order to restrain him or her. Keep your hold firm, talking all the time to help calm the child down, if necessary until the storm of emotions has passed. This is an effective way to communicate that physical violence is not acceptable, without you losing your own temper and becoming violent yourself. This can only work if you remain calm, clear and in control of the situation yourself.
- As far as possible try to remain out of your children's quarrels and let them sort them out themselves. They won't learn how to resolve conflict if you constantly jump in and deal with it. It can, of course, be painful to overhear the verbal abuse that youngsters often indulge in, but console yourself by remembering that these words often don't carry the same power as they do for adults, that their feelings are better expressed than suppressed and that children are remarkably resilient and forgiving and forget the conflict very quickly.
- In spite of this, however, there are occasions when you can identify the warning signs of an escalating conflict, when it is wise to step in before things really get out of hand. In such situations, it can be better to use a distraction technique or another way of defusing a potentially risky battle for your sake, as well as the children's.
- If the children are being really awful and refuse to get along together, try separating them into different rooms for a period. Tell them why you're doing this and that they can play together when they feel ready to be in a better mood with each other. Don't look on this as a punishment, but more as a breathing space for everyone concerned. They can amuse themselves while they're on their own.
- If you can't separate them for some reason, and you're getting really

wound up, try isolating *yourself* for a while. It can work wonders to go into another room to calm down and let them get on with it. Take a deep breath, count to ten or a hundred, play some music, lie down, watch television, or read a pleasant book. Or go and do gardening or, if there's another adult around or the children are old enough to be left on their own for a short time, take a brisk walk until you feel ready to face things at home again. Preserving your sanity is essential and the calmer and more in control you are, the better parent to them you'll be.

- It may seem obvious, but it's worth remembering that grown-ups frequently only pay attention to children when things are going wrong. When they're getting on well together, we may ignore them, just thankful for the peace and quiet, but forgetting to let them know how much we appreciate their behaviour. Giving children attention when they're doing what we don't want is called 'negative reinforcement' and means we actually are making it more likely that they'll repeat this behaviour. To encourage the behaviour we do want, such as playing happily together, we need to switch to 'positive reinforcement' – that is, commenting on and appreciating it, using phrases like: 'I feel so happy when I see you and Mark playing together like this. You both seem to be enjoying yourselves a lot and really having fun.'

- If you don't want your children to use violence towards each other, then it's important not to use it yourself with them, either. If you use hitting and smacking, you automatically give them 'permission' to use it. It cannot be fair to children to say that it's OK for you to use violence, but not for them to use it.

- Many parents set themselves high standards and get upset when they don't meet them, because they've lost control and have perhaps behaved in a way they regret with their children. One way to help children learn how to acknowledge another person's hurt and to apologise with dignity is by seeing you do it. A statement like: 'I feel very upset about losing my temper with you just now. I was angry, but I'm not any more and I want to make friends again . . .' can show your children that pride need not get in the way of making amends. So try not to be too proud to say 'Sorry' yourself to your youngsters. It lets them know you aren't infallible and sets an example of flexibility and openness to them as well.

- Finally, if you find that fighting tends to happen at predictable times of the day, it's sensible to review these and see if you can make any changes. Early morning when there's a rush to get breakfast, washed, dressed and so on is typically a time when tempers rise. It also happens in the evenings, when family members are perhaps hungry before a meal is ready, or tired at the end of a long day. Changing your routine a little can often help to reduce or prevent friction between your youngsters, as we saw earlier in Alison's case.

PLEASURES OF THE SAME AND OPPOSITE SEX SIBLINGS

Earlier in this chapter we looked at the special problems of sibling rivalry between boys and girls, but it's worth mentioning that there are also certain pleasures to be had from siblings of the same and opposite sex. For example, Mandy, whose two daughters are now grown up, says that when they were younger they used to fight a great deal, but they were also very close and protective towards each other. But now, as she reports:

> They rarely quarrel. Of course, they're no longer living at home and they each have their own places about fifteen minutes apart in London and that probably makes a difference. But now they're great friends and share a lot with each other. They meet regularly, at least once a week, which is more than I see them, and they're always chatting on the phone to each other. I feel sure they wouldn't be as close if they were opposite sex siblings.

Planning family activities is probably easier if you have siblings of the same sex, sometimes at least. Choosing a film, deciding which museum to visit or organising a day out is likely to be easier if there aren't disagreements over one child wanting to watch a football match while another wants a new party outfit.

The advantages of siblings of the same sex can be more apparent as they move into adolescence when there is a tendency to withdraw from the adult world into a special secret world of teenagers. Many teenage girls share fantasies about pop singers and film or television actors, that they can't share with their brothers. And they enjoy talking about their particular interests together, as well as the typical 'feminine' ones that preoccupy so many at this stage in life.

And teenage boys can share sporting activities or others that are considered to fall in the 'masculine' realm with each other in a similar way. Many parents report that families made up just of boys seem to be noisier and more boisterous right through the age spectrum, as Mandy describes:

> My sister had two boys who were always getting into scrapes and always seemed to be grubby from their football or cricket games. But both my daughters and my brother's daughters were much quieter in this respect and I feel we had an easier time with girls than my sister had with her boys. And now I have two teenage stepsons who leap round the house incredibly noisily and fool around no end, so I do feel that boys are generally louder and more active.

SEX AND SIBLINGS

Most of us can remember from our own childhood our curiosity and fascination with sex. If you had siblings, the chances are that you played games like 'mothers and fathers' or 'doctors and nurses' which involved exploring each other's bodies, as well as imitating adult roles.

This childish curiosity is normal and quite natural, as is masturbation. However, many parents are quite shocked when they discover their children's interest in sexual matters and their reactions often unintentionally communicate a sense of guilt or shame to their children.

Balancing the realisation that masturbation and sex play are a normal part of growing up with wanting to teach your child that certain parts of his or her body are 'private' is not always easy. The recent publicity and concern with sexual abuse in families has led many parents to take an active stance in helping their youngsters to protect themselves from unwanted sexual attention from older relatives and strangers (almost always male).

Joanna expressed her concern for her two small children as follows:

> Judging from the children I know, they're all fascinated with each other! Since I'm trying to give Sally the idea that her bottom is private and hers, I discourage her from playing with Richard's willy (with which she's fascinated) on the grounds that it's his, and also private.

Children who grow up familiar with the sexual differences between males and females as a result of natural contact with their siblings' and parents' bodies without shame or guilt are much less likely to be curious in a secretive or prurient manner with each other or their friends. Frank and simple answers to children's questions about where they come from and how they grew in their mother's tummy lay the foundation for a healthy knowledge of sex as they mature.

If you discover your children engaged in masturbation or sex play or exploration, the best way of dealing with it is matter-of-factly, without shock, exaggeration or indignation. You can explain that these things are not done in public and distract their attention with other activities. Supervision is the best solution and punishment should always be avoided, as it inevitably leads to feelings of guilt and shame developing.

As your children grow older, it's wise as far as possible to arrange their bedrooms so that only youngsters of the same sex share the same room. It's quite natural for them to creep into each other's beds for warmth, comfort or amusement and if boys and girls share the same room, there's a greater chance of encouraging sex games inadvertently.

It sometimes happens that an older brother engages in sexual or pseudo-sexual activities with a younger sister, and the results of this can be very damaging and long lasting. This is particularly true where the girl feels she cannot tell her parents because of feelings of guilt, shame or secrecy, or because of the fear of reprisals from the older brother.

If you discover that something like this has been happening with your children, it's essential to deal with it immediately. The best policy is a firm and quiet talk with your son, explaining that this kind of sexual behaviour is completely unacceptable in any form and that genital contact with a young girl is very painful and injurious. Depending on the age of your son, it's a good idea to appeal to his common sense and compassion. Explain that it's not fair to impose his advances on his sister and nor is it permissible to use persuasion or force to get his way.

As a general guide, remember that the more trust, openness and respect there exists in your family, the less likelihood there is of any damage being caused to your children by the normal sexual curiosity of childhood. If you are worried about any aspect of your children's sexuality or development, don't hesitate to get professional help. Your GP or health visitor are usually the best people to advise you in the first instance.

CHILDREN IN STEPFAMILIES

The problems of bringing up children in a family can be complicated enough when they share the same parents, but things can become far more complicated in the 're-formed' families that result from the death of a spouse, or – much more commonly – separation and divorce.

There are many thousands of stepfamilies in Britain today and the numbers are increasing, with the rising divorce rate. Most divorcees remarry sooner or later and these remarriages may involve one or several children from either partner's previous marriage, as well as a new child from the present relationship.

The subject of stepfamilies and the complex relationships that result is beyond the scope of this book apart from a couple of pointers. First, it's important to remember that stepfamilies take a long time – perhaps years – to settle in and develop the kind of family unity and loyalty the parents so often desire. And in many cases, it's best to be realistic and be aware that these things may never be possible, simply because the children have their own loyalties and affections and will not be diverted just because a parent wants things to be different.

The children of the previous marriage may be deeply resentful of the changes forced upon them as a result of the divorce. They are often hostile or jealous of the new partner and may have powerful similar feelings about any stepsiblings.

Living in a stepfamily relationship can make enormous demands on the maturity and patience of the couple concerned and certainly makes it more difficult for them to settle into their own relationship, unlike the average newlywed pair. Because of the extra pressures, such couples are under particular stress and this is unlikely to be eased by the arrival of a new baby, no matter how much he or she may have been wanted to consolidate the new relationship.

There are many variations on the stepfamily relationship, including those where the children of both parties all live together, where those of one partner stay with the previous spouse, and where there are weekend or holiday stepfamilies because of access agreements, to mention just a few examples.

Many of the tips and guidelines mentioned earlier in this chapter are relevant for children in stepfamilies. But there may be occasions when you feel that your problems are unique and you want extra support or advice. At times like these it's worth contacting 'Stepfamily', which is the national association to support stepfamilies and has local branches around the country (see p 114 in Appendix II for details).

And if your problems are really beyond the scope of voluntary counselling and support, you may be better off seeking help from an organisation like Relate or to opt for family therapy to help sort out what is going wrong.

FAVOURITISM QUESTIONNAIRE

Do you prefer one of your children to another? You may not realise that you do, so here's a checklist of questions:

1. Do you find that you tend to give one of your youngsters more time, attention or gifts than another?
2. Do you see a special resemblance between yourself and a particular child?
3. If so, do you often comment on it, either to the child concerned or to other people?
4. Do you tend to be more strict or punish one of your children more, or to be more permissive with another?
5. Does one of your children play up more than another? If so, check to see whether she feels she has to do this to get your attention.
6. Does one of your children tend to annoy you more than another?
7. Do you enjoy the company of one child more than another's?
8. Do you feel particularly close to a child who's the same position in the family as you were in yours?
9. Do you have a favourite child in the family that you know of – and does your partner, too? If you do, does this lead to friction between you or the children concerned?
10. Was a particular child a much longed for baby – perhaps born after a long period of trying, or a child of a much wanted sex?

Tips on coping with favouritism in the family

- If your answers to any of these questions lead you to think you favour a particular child, try to discover the reason why. For example, you may feel closer to your daughter simply because she is female, or to your oldest child because you were the oldest, too.
- Do listen to a child that complains of your favouritism. It doesn't necessarily mean it's true, but at least take it seriously and try to understand why he or she *feels* this way. Don't laugh at, dismiss or ridicule a child who feels unfairly treated.
- It's important to realise that any favouritism in the family soon leads to anger and resentment on the part of other children. This can become a vicious circle, with difficult behaviour leading you to dislike the child even more. So try to break this circle as soon as possible.
- Try to compensate for your feelings of favouritism with the less favoured child(ren). Give time, attention and small gifts to help make up for the feelings of unfairness.
- Try to look for all the positive qualities in a child who's being difficult to like for the time being. Keep things in perspective and remember that this is a stage that will soon pass.
- Remember that 'bad' or difficult behaviour is usually a sign of distress or a cry for help from a child who doesn't know how to get what she needs in another way.

- If you and your partner do have your own favourites, try swapping them over for outings and other activities. It's vital to make your own special relationship with each child, independently of other members of the family, and to communicate that you love your childen for *who* they are.
- Share your feelings about favouritism with your partner and ask for help in coping with them.
- If you find the problem is too big for you to deal with on your own, don't be afraid to talk to a counsellor or other skilled person to help you sort things out.

5 Partners and fathers

So far in this book, we've been talking about having a second (or third) baby mainly from the mother's point of view. But of course, much of what we've said applies to men, as well. In this chapter, however, we want to look at the special role and contribution of men, both as fathers and partners. So, in this chapter, we use the word 'you' to mean the father and partner.

THE FATHER'S ROLE

For the last hundred years or so, ever since theories on child development and psychoanalysis have been developed, most of the emphasis has been on the mother's influence on her children – not only in their early years, but right through adult life. It's only in the last ten or fifteen years that much attention has been paid to the father's role.

It used to be thought that only mothers were biologically adapted to bringing up children – and indeed, many people still cling to this belief. There is, however, ample evidence from research into human and animal child-rearing patterns to question this idea. Experts who have studied families in recent years have found, not unexpectedly, that many fathers are as important to their children as their mother, and are becoming increasingly involved in caring for their children. And single fathers who take all the responsibility for their children's daily care are a small but growing minority.

Studies of fathers and babies have also shown that men are just as good as women at understanding and responding to a baby's cry, giving a bottle-feed, talking to their baby and playing with him. Most babies soon become closely attached to their father as well as their mother. They are delighted when he comes home and by the age of eighteen months, most babies protest equally at either parent leaving the room.

The main problem is that most fathers, and many mothers too, don't *believe* that they can do it. A recent study in Australia found that nearly three out of four fathers (and half of the mothers) believed that women have a natural 'maternal instinct' which fathers lack. Although two out of three mothers believed that their husbands were quite capable of looking after the children, only one in the three fathers believed they could do it.

These studies also show that fathers tend to spend more time *playing* with their children and are more likely to play active, physical games (especially with boys). Because play is vital to the way a child learns and grows, a father's active involvement – or the lack of it – can have a big effect.

So fathers need to realise that they do matter to their children's development, right from the beginning. The Cambridge survey already mentioned on page 14 showed, for instance, that things are often much easier after the second baby is born if the father has already developed a close relationship with the older child.

We believe that fathers are just as important in their children's lives and development as mothers are. This is true even though your role may be different and your opportunity for active parenting may be more limited because of work and social pressures. In this chapter, we look at how you and your partner can decide what kind of parents you both want to be, how you can play an active part in bringing up your children – and how you can maintain a happy partnership, too.

PREGNANCY THE SECOND TIME ROUND

Many fathers remember the excitement – and often the apprehension – they felt when their partner was pregnant with their first baby. For both of you, that first pregnancy was a time of discovery. And if you were present at your baby's birth, you're unlikely ever to forget it.

The second time round, it's easy to be much more matter-of-fact about your partner's pregnancy and the forthcoming birth. If everything went reasonably well, you probably feel that there's less to worry about this time, too. And having to combine a job with helping to bring up your first child, you and your partner probably don't have a great deal of time to talk or think much about this pregnancy.

But, surprisingly perhaps, your partner may need *more* support in this pregnancy than she did before. It's true that it's no longer a new experience, but she's almost certainly more tired. She may be suffering from sickness and the usual fatigue that's so common in pregnancy. And with an older child to care for – perhaps a very lively toddler – she has little time to get the extra rest and sleep which both she and the growing baby need.

It might help to think back to what you did during the first pregnancy. Did you go with your partner to her clinic visits or to the childbirth preparation classes? Did you make sure she took some rest at the weekend when you were at home to take over from her? Did you do more of the shopping, cooking and cleaning? It is probably very helpful to talk to your partner about what she would really like you to do this time round. It's possible that with a first baby your employer was more sympathetic to the idea of your taking time off during your partner's pregnancy than he is this time, but she won't know that unless you discuss it with her.

As we mentioned earlier, one of the striking findings of the Cambridge survey was that there is often less conflict between the first child and the mother after the second baby is born, if the older child already has a close relationship with the father. So one of the most important things you can do during this second pregnancy is to spend as much time as possible with your child.

Another study found that babies who have a secure and loving relationship with *both* their father and mother are more sociable than those who have a secure relationship with their mother only. So apart from anything else, this is another good reason for making sure you're close to your older child – and later on to your other children, too, of course.

If you don't have this close relationship already established, it's possible that your child may feel rejected or pushed out of the way from his mother to make room for the new baby. He may feel that he's being 'fobbed off' on to you to be looked after so that this important newcomer can take his place. So now is the ideal time to begin to develop the kind of relationship you want with your first child, if you haven't done so already. You may, of course, already have a settled routine of things you do together. So if you're already in a close relationship, it will be easy to develop it still further.

It often happens that fathers feel their child is closer to his mother than to them, and that she is the expert at coping with all of his needs. It's likely that your partner already has a network of other mothers who are her friends. So you may not be as involved in bringing up your child as you'd like to be. You can change this, now while your child is still young, even though you may be working long hours in a more than full-time job or career. There are always the evenings or the weekends, depending on your work schedule.

Ideally, you will be able to arrange time with your child in a way that also gives your partner some time off to rest. If she is feeling tired and ill, especially in early pregnancy, or particularly exhausted in the later months, it can make all the difference if you get your child up and dressed in the morning and organise breakfast for all of you. Another idea is to take over the weekly shopping trip by making it an outing for you and your youngster, while your partner takes a nap.

There are many ways to reorganise your routine at home so that you can combine child care with taking over other domestic tasks from your partner. The exact way in which you do this will depend on your particular circumstances and what you and your partner need most right now. What matters most, however, is that you pull together and put the time in at this point.

If you have friends with small children, it's a nice idea to get together with them to organise outings as a group. It's certainly more enjoyable than being on your own and it's less tiring, too. Your partner is likely to know of other women who are pregnant for the second time round, too, and she could ask if their partners would like to team up to share a trip to the local playground, swimming pool and so on with you.

Women have a special advantage in this respect, since they get to know other mothers with small children through their local clinics, mother and toddler groups, playgroups and so on. Men don't usually have this kind of opportunity to establish a support network for themselves but it's certainly worth trying and asking your partner for her ideas and help.

Some fathers can feel quite excluded from caring for their children as a result of their partner's skill and experience in handling them. Mothers are also the only ones who can breastfeed. Your partner may have gone back to work after taking some time off to have the first baby, but even so she will have had time to get to know the baby and to develop all the practical skills of feeding, bathing, nappy-changing, dressing and organising the routine around his needs.

By the time a second or third child arrives, the mother is usually so competent that she may make her partner feel clumsy or inadequate when he tries to help with simple things like settling a fractious child down to sleep. Many mothers are keen to have their partner's help with a baby or toddler, but they often get quite irritated or impatient with his efforts to cope.

If you feel this applies to you, try talking it over quietly with your partner to explain how you feel. It's not your fault that you're not as accomplished in the art of child care, but you certainly can learn and practice will help to make you faster and more skilled. It may irritate her to see you packing a baby bag slowly and asking what's needed, when she could do it all in a couple of minutes, but it's in her interests after all to give you the chance to learn!

WHEN THE BABY IS BORN

If you were present at your first child's birth, you'll probably want to be there again the second time. You may want to read the earlier chapters in this book about preparing your child and organising people to take care of him during the birth (see page 29).

If you weren't present at the birth the first time, you need to decide whether you would like to be there this time. Until about ten or fifteen years ago, it was common practice for hospitals to exclude fathers from the birth of their babies. Today, things are completely different and it's now considered unusual for a father not to be present. Fathers are encouraged to be in the labour ward and to play an active part, including massaging their partner's back, supporting her if she's in an upright position, helping to deliver the baby and holding the baby soon afterwards. Research in both Britain and the USA indicates that the great majority of fathers who are present at the birth are enthusiastic about the whole experience.

If you would like more information about how you can help your partner through the pregnancy and the delivery, one of the best books is *Childbirth for Men* by Herbert Brandt, Professor of Gynaecology at University College Hospital, London. (One expectant father who asked for a copy at the medical bookshop near the hospital was told to look for it in the section on 'Miracles'!)

TIME OFF FOR FATHERS

The idea of paid time off from work for mothers when they have a baby is now recognised by law, even though the conditions are so restrictive in practice that only half of them actually qualify. But fathers have no such rights at all.

There are a few employers, such as local councils and some publishing firms, that do accept that a father needs to be able to put his family first when a new baby is born. In Sweden, however, a father is entitled to two weeks' paternity leave for the birth of a child. Both father and mother are entitled to share a further twelve months' paid leave between them and in 1991 this will be increased to eighteen months' leave. After the parental leave period ends, either parent is entitled to shorten their working hours, with a corresponding reduction in salary, until their child is eight years old.

The parents can also take up to ninety days off a year for family reasons, such as a child's illness, school visits and so on. In practice, however, very few parents use up so much time. British employers argue that the cost of establishing paternity leave as a right for all fathers would be prohibitive, but this certainly has not happened in Sweden, where the economy is thriving!

The European Community, too, has included paternity leave in its proposed 'Social Charter' and in a draft, 'Directive on Parental Leave'. Unfortunately the British government has so far rejected both of these.

If your employer doesn't provide paternity leave as a matter of course, you may be able to negotiate an individual arrangement. If you are a member of a trade union you should discuss it with your union representative and try to get a general provision on paternity leave agreed with the employer. Any such agreement should, if possible, include a right to attend preparation for childbirth classes, which is the equivalent of a mother's legal right to paid time off for antenatal appointments. You should also try to negotiate at least one or two weeks off work at the time of the baby's birth.

Apart from the objection from employers that this kind of leave for male staff would cost far too much, there is also the argument that it would be difficult or impossible to reallocate a man's work during his absence. You even hear it argued that there might be two men both claiming paternity leave from different employers for the same baby as an objection to the idea!

However, these arguments simply don't stand up to scrutiny. If you find yourself in the position of arguing your case for paternity leave, you might like to consider using one or all of the following points:

1. Women have a statutory legal right to paid time off for antenatal care and when they have a baby. In these days of non-discrimination and equal opportunities, men ought to have an equivalent right.
2. Paternity leave is much less expensive than maternity leave. Two weeks' paid leave when the baby is born, plus (say) two half-days off for childbirth classes will only cost the employer eleven days' pay. A woman's legal rights could include six days or more for antenatal visits, as well as six weeks' paid maternity leave.
3. Organising someone to cover for you during two weeks' paternity leave is much less of a burden than coping with annual holidays (which are now around five weeks a year, on average) or with maternity leave. A woman who has had a baby is entitled to return to her job up to twenty-nine weeks afterwards (even though she is not paid for most of this period).
4. It takes two to make a baby. Doctors and psychologists recognise the father's vital role in supporting the mother during pregnancy and childbirth – and employers need to recognise it too, just as they recognise the mother's role.
5. At a more practical level, both the government and employers want to encourage women back into paid employment, and this means that men will have to take on more responsibility at home. Norman Fowler, the former Secretary of State for Employment, said that men would need to do more of the housework if women were to do more of the jobs. Sharing the responsibility for children starts when they are born.
6. Finally, neither you nor your partner will be getting much sleep during the baby's early weeks at home. You won't be at your best at work and if you have to draw on your holiday entitlement now, you won't get the rest you need later in the year. Your employer will get more out of you if you're not exhausted.

If these arguments don't work, you will have to use part of your holiday and decide with your partner how much time you need to have when the baby is born, and how much you want to keep for a family holiday later.

WHAT KIND OF FATHER DO YOU WANT TO BE?

It's often argued that the role of being a mother is greatly undervalued in our society. But the role of father is perhaps given even less recognition, except as the breadwinner whose job it is to work as hard as possible to make sure there's enough money coming into the home.

The early years of family life are very expensive. If your partner gives up work or changes over to a part-time job, there's bound to be less money coming in. And if she goes back to work, you'll have to find the money to pay for child care and possibly other domestic help. Either way, there are also extra costs of baby equipment and perhaps higher rent or mortgage for larger accommodation for your growing family. Because it's assumed that men will take financial responsibility for their family, the economic pressures can be quite tough on you.

Combining work and family life and trying to get a reasonable balance between them can be quite difficult, just as it is for your partner. You probably want to be with your children most when they're young and yet this is the time when you have to work the hardest. You may need to work long hours of overtime or to take on extra responsibilities to develop your career in order to satisfy the need for a higher income to support your growing family.

So no matter how committed both you and your partner are to sharing the pleasures and responsibilities of bringing up children, you may find that in practice the balance is hard to achieve. Before you had children, you were both earning and contributing more or less equally to the household. But by the time your second or third child has arrived, the division of work is probably well established, with your partner as the one who takes care of the home and the children, and you as the family breadwinner.

The arrival of a second baby offers an ideal opportunity for you and your partner to talk about whether you're happy with the way your life and relationship are working out for both of you. For most couples, having a family is an important part of their relationship with their partner. But few couples ever talk about what kind of parents they want to be before their first child is born – or whether they want to change things when their second child arrives.

Most of us go into parenthood with fairly hazy ideas of what it will really be like on a day-to-day basis. Sometimes, we may have fantasies about being an ideal family with rosy-cheeked spotless children who never cause a moment's trouble. So the reality often comes as quite a shock when you find yourselves having to cope with a tiny, demanding bundle who refuses to delay having his needs satisfied and who turns your nice orderly routine upside-down.

It's rare indeed for couples to talk about the practicalities of managing the daily care for the first baby and most assume that it is the mother's role to look after this side of things at home. By the time the second baby arrives, most couples have settled into some sort of domestic rhythm, which is again disturbed by the newcomer.

If you're happy with the pattern you developed with your first child, then it should be fairly easy to adapt to having two children. Earlier chapters in this book offer some practical guidance on how to deal with the particular problems you may encounter.

If you want to change things so that you can be more involved with your children, then you will have to decide whether fairly small changes in your routine will be enough, or whether something more drastic is called for. For instance, you may want to spend more time together as a family, or have time by yourself with one or both children. Reorganising your evenings and weekends could help here. The section on 'time' in the next chapter (see page 100) may give you some useful ideas.

On the other hand, you may decide that you want to spend much more time with your children while they are very young. Although a growing number of women do earn more than their partners, men's average earnings are still about one-quarter higher than women's. So if you both decide to work part-time, for instance, it could mean quite a drop in your family income. The scope for changing your working hours obviously depends on the kind of work you do; whether you can reduce your overtime or allow your career to progress more slowly for a few years.

One couple we know decided to reorganise their working lives after their second child arrived. They did this by each working three days a week and arranging for a childminder to look after the children on the one day they were both at work. This meant that they had more money than one of them would have earned on the basis of one salary and they had only to pay for one day's child care. And they both felt they were contributing financially and had the advantage of keeping in touch with the outside world through their jobs. From the woman's point of view in this case, it meant she had a wider horizon than simply home and children and this was good for their relationship, too.

YOUR RELATIONSHIP WITH YOUR PARTNER

Having a second or third baby can place even more strain on your partnership than having a first. If you have the children close together, the chances of getting enough sleep are lessened, which means that you're more likely to be irritable with each other. Coping with the demands of a jealous older child can be tricky, too, and all things considered, it's remarkable that so many couples do manage to weather the storm of the early years of parenthood so successfully.

If you're working full time, not getting enough sleep and perhaps worrying about money as well, then you may not have much energy at the end of the day to talk to your partner and listen to her as well. For your partner, coping with two or three small children full time, or combining motherhood with a job and running the home, this stage in your growing family's life is probably the most demanding and exhausting, too.

In many marriages this is a very critical time. It's now that you most need to stay close to each other – but it's also the period when this is most difficult to achieve. You may find yourselves beginning to lead rather separate lives – not because you want to, but simply because you don't realise it's happening. After all, the children's needs come first, or so most of us believe. Sacrifices are part of parenthood, and if your own parents sacrificed a great deal for you, you may believe that this is the right way to relate to your own children.

The problem with this attitude is that if you put your relationship with your partner in second place to your children's needs, your relationship may eventually suffer permanent damage. And, needless to say, if the marriage is unhappy, then the children will suffer, too.

You may feel you're carrying most or all of the family's financial burden. If you return to an untidy home, with late meals, an exhausted partner and squabbling children, you could be forgiven for thinking this is not what family life was meant to be like. You may feel that your partner has no time for you any more and that she's more concerned with the children than with you. And it's quite common for a father to feel jealous of a new baby, particularly if his partner no longer seems to be interested in making love with him.

Many men accept this feeling of exclusion with resignation, hoping that things will improve as time goes by. But some find themselves becoming angry or resentful or even threatened. And they may find it very difficult to put these feelings into words, in spite of the fact that they may be very powerful, because they're not the sort of feelings that people talk about in everyday conversation. After all, you've achieved your ambition of marriage and setting up a home together and then starting your longed-for family. So you should be feeling happy and fulfilled in your role as a father.

Because you may be in conflict over feelings like this, it can seem easier to shut down and avoid talking about them altogether. Retreating into silence or disappearing behind the newspaper in front of the television are ways of escaping difficulties of this kind, but it's a good idea to look at the situation from your partner's point of view, too. She may know that you're having to work long hours in order to earn the money you all need. But at the same time, she may feel emotionally abandoned because you never seem to be there to share the children's lives with her. If you appear not to have the time or energy to talk, she may become increasingly resentful and angry in her turn.

So you need to find time to talk to each other. You also need to make time for yourself. We discuss the problem of organising your time in detail in Chapter 6 (see page 100). Some couples organise things so that each of them has an evening off during the week, while the other looks after the children. That way, you can get an evening alone with your children, and you both get an evening to yourself.

Alistair is the father of five sons and has been through most of the typical ups and downs of family life. He has found a way to make more time for himself combined with getting to know his children as individuals:

> Now the boys are a bit older, I'm going to do something which a friend of mine has been doing with his children and take each child out to dinner or the theatre, or something like that – just each one on his own. It seems to be a good way of getting to know your children as individuals as they're growing up – and anyway I'll enjoy it, too!

MAKING TIME TOGETHER

Time for each other is just as important – time to talk things over between you, to laugh together, to cry and share sadness with each other, time for your own growth and development as a couple, and not simply as mother and father. This can sound a tall order when your time and money are so limited anyway. But it can be done.

Some couples make sure they have an hour or two together at the end of each day. Mandy talks about how she and Jim feel:

> I find if we don't get an hour or two each day together away from work and children, than I get miserable and irritable. It doesn't mean we have to go out – usually we talk together in bed when the house is

quiet and it cements our closeness and helps us to feel in contact with each other much more deeply. I value this time for us above everything else and I'm certain that we stay sane and balanced because of it.

Getting an evening on your own together regularly, without the children, is very important. If you didn't get into that habit after your first baby was born, it's important to do it now. After all, once your youngest baby is old enough to be left, a relative or babysitter can cope almost as easily with two or three children as with one.

If you're a stepfamily, then time together may be even more important, as Corinne explains:

> Bob has a son from his previous marriage and I have two boys from mine. We also have a little girl of our own, so we're quite a tribe on holiday together and the relationships aren't always easy, to say the least! We find it essential to make time for ourselves occasionally and to have all the children looked after so that we can make contact with each other and try to remember why we got married to each other in the first place!

PARENTHOOD AND PARTNERSHIP

It's important to remember that parenthood is primarily about partnership and the couple who keep their relationship alive and in good shape is likely to survive the storms they inevitably meet. This means that both partners have to believe in themselves in their respective roles as mother and father and in their ability to cope with whatever crops up.

They also need to have faith in each other and to be able to affirm each other as lovers, friends, spouses and as parents. Even when they disagree, as every couple does at times, they need to be able to handle their conflicts creatively and constructively in a spirit of goodwill.

This point about disagreement is particularly important with regard to basic beliefs and values about the way your children are to brought up. All too often, couples don't consider these issues except in a sketchy way before the arrival of the first child. But as the family grows, all sorts of issues arise that can lead to conflict between parents, including things like standards of behaviour at home, tidiness, discipline and punishment, religion, education and so on.

These disagreements can become even greater when the children reach the teenage years. By then they are beginning to develop their own beliefs and standards which may be at odds with their parents' and include thorny subjects like sex, hairstyles, clothes, friendships, politics, music and so on.

There can be considerable disagreement between some couples, as happens in mixed marriages with differences of race or religious belief, for example. Marriages between British and Asian, Catholic and Protestant, Jew and Christian, Turkish and Scots are found from time to time or, as with one couple we know, between Indian Sikh and Irish Catholic. Such differences *can* be continued as long as there is tolerance and respect for each partner's religious belief or cultural background without either wanting their own to dominate in the relationship. And of course, it is even more important for the couple concerned to be flexible because the stresses inside the marriage are likely to be greater, as well as the attitudes and prejudices of other people which can create their own problems.

A couple in this situation needs also to work out which faith the children of the marriage are to be raised in and to be able to explain their differences clearly to them as they grow up. But if there is unresolved conflict in the relationship, it's likely that these differences can become the triggers for further rifts that may eventually tear the marriage apart.

So try to keep your feelings about each other positive through all the ups and downs and keep the channels of communication open. In this way both of you can develop the trust and respect that's so essential for your partnership to endure. It's also vital for your relationship with your children, for they will model themselves on how you behave towards each other.

Remember that both of you will be going through enormous changes in the years ahead and that you need to make allowances for each other, too. Try to take account of your partner's tiredness as well as your own, and the need to let domestic standards slip if necessary to allow for the demands and pressures of young children.

Because of the impact of these changes in your life, you will probably experience times when it's hard to cope with your feelings. Perhaps it isn't surprising that some fathers retreat into spending more and more time with other men, at the pub in the evenings or watching sport at weekends. Others become workaholics with the perfect excuse of having to work harder to provide for the family. And some look to an affair with another woman to supply the affection they feel they're not getting at home.

All of these are warning signs that things are going wrong between you. You need to stop and talk about what is happening. Many couples find it easier to face up to conflicts between them if they get some help from an experienced counsellor or therapist as Lorraine describes:

> Martin and I were having enormous problems in our marriage and actually split up for three months. He was buried in his work, which meant I felt he wasn't emotionally available for me and I had an affair. We decided to try for a reconciliation and went for counselling. We saw our therapists separately and together, and as a result we were able to understand far more clearly what had been happening between us. Our relationship is much stronger now than it has ever been in the ten years we've been together.

YOUR SEXUAL RELATIONSHIP

Sadly, as many couples discover, having young children can ruin your sex life. Sleepless nights and long working hours for both of you – at home or in a job – can wreak havoc with your sexual drive. You may have already dealt with this problem after the birth of your first child, in which case it should be easier the second time.

But if you didn't get back into a satisfactory sexual relationship, then having a second child can make this particular problem worse. Because sexual frustration and the feeling that your partner is rejecting you can build up into resentment and anger that eventually destroys a relationship completely, it's vital to sort things out before it gets too late.

It is most important to talk about how you both feel. You may both decide that, given the demands of family and work, you don't want to make love as often as you used to. Agreeing on a less active sexual relationship, or settling for something you both feel is less than perfect, may be the right thing for you at this stage. But if you don't talk about it at all and just ignore the situation, you're likely to be storing up trouble for the future. Many family therapists and counsellors say that a couple's sexual relationship is a sensitive barometer of the rest of their relationship and that if this isn't working, then they're likely to be having other problems, too.

Many men find it particularly difficult to talk about their feelings. Powerful cultural barriers still exist which prevent emotional expression by boys and men. Again, family counsellors often find that the problems which occur over and over again in relationships centre round the inability of one or both partners to talk about their deeper feelings.

One of the biggest complaints that many women make about their partners is lack of emotional availability. You may feel embarrassed at discussing your feelings, or you may believe, as many people do, that talking about emotions creates problems that will go away if they're not put into words. Your partner is more likely to see your unwillingness to talk as rejection of her and withdrawal from your relationship together.

Adults who go to a therapist or counsellor often discover, as they explore their relationships with their own parents, that they feel enormous pain and anger at their father's emotional absence and their own inability, as children, to get near him. Jack, who is now the father of three himself, speaks for many men when he says:

> I never knew my father as a real person. He always felt distant from me. I knew he was there in the background and I suppose he loved me because he worked very hard to keep us all. But I never felt he really loved me with his heart and soul. He simply didn't know how to communicate his feelings to us at all.

The more you can express your feelings with your partner, the better you'll be able to communicate your love for your children. Emotional expression doesn't just come through words and saying things like 'I love you' or 'I appreciate you', although these are indeed very important. It also comes through your eye contact, through touch, hugs, kisses and many other forms of physical warmth and contact. Your children will absorb this behaviour between you and your partner until it becomes part of their own standards and expectations of the relationships they will make in the future.

One of the most fascinating parts of becoming a parent for both men and women is the way the experience changes our relationships with other members of our family. It's common, for example, for first- or second-time parents to begin to express appreciation for their own parents, as Mandy describes here:

> When I became a mother, I was suddenly aware of a much greater recognition of my own parents – both my mother and father – and all their love and work for me and my brothers and sister. I stopped taking them for granted and saw them with new eyes as an adult and that was the beginning of a new stage in our relationship. And I know that other friends of mine – male and female – have gone through something similar in their own relationships with their parents, too.

Another dimension of parenthood that comes as a wonderful surprise is the miracle of watching small children grow up. Few of us begin to appreciate this until we become parents ourselves. The mother who parents alone – and that includes the woman whose partner is emotionally absent even though they live together – is deprived of the experience of sharing this at a deeper level. The father who does not take advantage of the opportunity to develop the most intimate relationship possible after that with his own partner is missing out on one of life's treasures, as well as the chance to forge a powerful influence that lasts well beyond the next generation.

6 Life with two – the practicalities

In this chapter, we look at some of the *practical* problems involved in life with two or more children. There are no 'right' and 'wrong' ways of dealing with these problems: just ways that work for you and your family. But it's helpful to know how other parents have coped and to learn from their experience.

TIME

One of the toughest problems for parents of two or more children is finding the time you need. Not just time for the baby as well as the older child or children, but time for yourselves – alone and together.

If, like most parents, you've found every twenty-four hours crowded enough with only one child, then it will be obvious that something has to give. In order to find a solution that will work for you, you need to think about *priorities* and you need to find *support*. And you need to do this with your partner – he's one of the priorities, but he's also a vital part of your support system!

PRIORITIES

An Australian family therapist, Steve Biddulph, who's written a bestselling book called *The Secret of Happy Families* startled many of his readers (including us) by saying that your priorities, as a mother, ought to be:

you
your partner
your children.

And yet, it makes sense. If you're exhausted, overworked and depressed, constantly trying to juggle an impossible set of demands, then you're not going to be a good mother. You need sleep, time for yourself and emotional support. And you need time with your partner, to keep your relationship alive and growing. With a very young baby and growing children, you won't get enough of what you need all the time, and there will always be bad patches, but over a period of several months or even a year you need to feel that your needs are being looked after too.

TIME WITH THE OLDER CHILD

Immediately after the birth of a new baby, the most pressing problem generally is to find time for both children. In many families, it's the older child who suffers. The Cambridge survey which we've referred to earlier found a startling drop in the time which mothers were able to spend with their first children after the second baby was born. Not surprisingly, the survey also found more conflict between mothers and first children.

1 am Cuddle
2:30 Feed/change
5 am Feed/change
5:30 Change
6:30 Cuddle
8 am Feed/change
8:30 Washing
9 am Feed/change/shops
11:30 Feed/change
2 noon Cuddle/feed
3 pm Feed/change
4:30 Doze/cuddle/feed
6 pm Bath/Feed/change
8-midnight walk up & down
12:30 Feed/change

Whatever happened to Four-hourly feeds?

And where do I fit in?

To start with, of course, your day will have to be rearranged around the new baby. But that doesn't mean that there can't be time for the older child too. Most babies need a great deal of sleep – even if they don't always sleep when their parents would like them to. For the first few weeks, if you still have someone to help with the older child, you're going to need to use at least some of the baby's daytime naps to catch up on your own sleep. But as things settle down, and you're on your own again, you may want to set aside at least one of your baby's naps and use the time for your older child.

Another way of using your baby's need to sleep is to take both children out to a local playcentre or a favourite park. Since fresh air and the rhythm of the pram or buggy helps to send most babies to sleep, you can then give your child undivided attention.

Another possibility, if your partner is at work during the day, is for him to spend time with the baby in the early evening, freeing you to look after the older child.

However you make the time, it should ideally be time just for you and her – not time when she's competing with the washing-up or cooking. If she knows that there will be some time in the day when you will do what *she* wants, it will make it easier for her to accept all those other times when the baby's needs get put first.

TIME WITH YOUR BABY

Of course, it isn't only your older child who needs your undivided attention occasionally. Your baby does too, so that you and he can get to know each other properly and so that he can develop the secure relationship with you on which he depends. It will make a very big difference if you can settle your child into a playgroup or nursery for an hour or two a day. If she is old enough, do try to organise this *before* the baby is born, so that she doesn't feel she's being pushed out of the house because of the baby. It's also much easier to get through any problems about separation before the new baby arrives, since you may find you need to stay at the playgroup with your child on several occasions before she settles happily enough to let you leave her there.

Joanna found that playgroup for her older daughter made a big difference to the whole family:

> Sally was too young to join any of the local playgroups before Richard was born. We went through a rough time for several months, when she was very jealous. When she was three and he was nineteen months, she got a place at the local playgroup for 2½ hours every day. She's much happier – she has new friends and new activities, she's much less jealous of Richard, she even comes home and teaches him all the little songs she's learnt. Somehow things at home are much less intense for her, and that makes it easier not just for her brother, but for us too.

Even a child who has settled happily at playgroup or nursery school may be unsettled by a new baby's arrival. One mother told us that her four-year-old suddenly refused to be left at the school which he had previously enjoyed, and tried to run away when she insisted on leaving him there. The problem was quickly solved, however, when she explained to him very carefully that there was plenty of room at home for both children, and he wouldn't come home to find that he'd been pushed out by the new baby.

You may already have a local network of babysitters who can help out occasionally. If you haven't, now is the time to develop it! Teenagers often make excellent babysitters for an evening out. A reliable teenager with experience of young children (perhaps her own siblings) might be able to take your older child out to a local playground for an hour after school. Or there might be an older woman living near you who would enjoy having your child to visit. Newsagents' noticeboards are a good way of finding babysitters, as well as checking the going rate for your area.

You may be lucky enough to have a mother, mother-in-law or other relative who can help. Or you could make an arrangement with another parent with children close in age to yours – so that she looks after her children and your older ones, while you get time with your baby. You can then do the same for her.

Whatever arrangement you're able to make, don't forget to let the babysitter know where you'll be and who else she can contact in an emergency. Explain how to use the telephone, radio, TV and video and let her know if you want her to answer the phone and take messages while you're away. And brief her carefully on your children's needs and routines, particularly for bedtime.

TIME FOR YOU

Even if you can manage to organise your day so that both children's needs are met, it's going to be difficult or impossible to cope with everything else that needs doing. As a result, most mothers of young families are desperately short of sleep. A recent survey found that over half of women said they were tired 'most of the time' (compared with only a quarter of the men).

If your older child still needs a daytime nap herself, you may be able to juggle sleep times so that for a blissful hour or so both children are asleep. The next step is to treat this brief interval as time for *you* – not time to catch up on the housework. If you're exhausted, physically and emotionally, from the non-stop demands of caring for children, a partner and a home, then you're not doing yourself or your children any good. Your first priority – hard though it sometimes is to believe – is to keep yourself well and happy. And that means using any time you can get to catch up on sleep, or read a book, or do whatever it is you need to recharge your own batteries.

TIME FOR YOURSELVES

As we stressed in the last chapter, it is terribly important to make time to be together, as a couple. You might want to have at least one evening a week out together: a babysitter can look after two children as easily (or almost as easily!) as one.

It is much more difficult to get, say, a weekend together without your children. But it is possible, and it is well worth it. One child may have been able to go and spend a day or two with a grandparent or aunt. With two or more children, it is generally easier to get the grandparent or aunt to come and stay with the children. Richard explained how he and Alison manage:

> We used to feel that it would be impossible to go away without the children. We thought they'd be miserable – and so would we. Then we tried it for a weekend, and my mum and dad came down to stay. The kids had a wonderful time, being spoilt rotten, and their grandparents adored having the children to themselves. In fact it's worked so well that we have now decided to take a week's holiday by ourselves.

AVOIDING THE 'SUPERMUM' TRAP

Looking after a new baby, finding some time for your older child and a little time for yourself inevitably means less time for other things. And that means *something has to go*. Most parents get by on less sleep than they used to get, but sacrificing your sleep in order to keep up with everything else you did previously is very unlikely to be the best choice.

So it makes sense to look at all the demands on your time and decide what matters to you most. It helps to write yourself a list – and perhaps even note down roughly how much time each activity takes. Just as you would do a budget for family finances, you can do a 'time budget' to help sort out your real priorities.

The more detailed you make your time budget, the easier it is to see if you are falling into the 'Supermum' trap.

We all know about Supermum. She not only has time to play creatively with her children, she makes most of their toys as well. Her meals are miniature works of art; even her cheese on toast is decorated with a face of sliced gherkins. She takes her children to playgroup, swimming and music lessons, and regularly entertains their friends to tea. If there's a fancy-dress party on, she creates a costume. She also makes many of their clothes. Her house is clean, her family's clothes are ironed, toys are tidied twice a day, and she even manages to shop for an elderly neighbour.

Supermum doesn't exist, except where it really matters, in the mind! To make matters even worse, she now has a sister – 'Executive Supermum'. Executive Supermum combines a high-powered and high-paid job with caring for her children and husband. The padded shoulders of her designer suits never seem to be stained from cuddling a small baby – or whipping up a three-course meal for entertaining business contacts!

In practice, of course, women who go back to part-time or full-time jobs after their babies are born spend most of their earnings on child care rather than clothes, and have as much difficulty as everyone else juggling the competing demands on their time.

One unfortunate result of the Supermum myth is that women today, on average, spend *more* time washing and ironing laundry than our grandmothers did sixty years ago, despite (or perhaps because of) all the modern appliances which are supposed to make life so convenient.

You can save time and escape the Supermum trap by doing *less* – less washing, less ironing, less cleaning, less cookery, less of whatever it is that takes up more time than you now have. You'll have to decide what it is that is going to go from your life. Get your partner involved in the decision too: after all, if he is really desperate to have his underpants ironed, he can always do them himself!

It can be surprisingly difficult to reduce your housework load. If you've always washed every item of your child's clothing after one wear, or ironed all her T-shirts, it may feel like giving up to let her wear the same trousers two days in a row (or three if you can get away with it!) and to leave the T-shirts crumpled. If you've always cooked a proper meal for yourself and your partner in the evenings, it may be hard to accept a cold snack or convenience food two or three or even five nights a week. Just keep asking yourself what is most important: time to read or play with your children, or keep yourself sane with half an hour's extra sleep, or spending more time on housework. You're not lowering your standards by cutting back, you're getting your priorities right.

SORTING OUT THE EVENINGS

Many families find the pressures get worse in the early evening, when everyone is tired. If you and your partner find this is when you're frequently snapping at each other, or having a serious argument, you need to stop and talk about what you each expect.

All too often, a father who comes home from work at the end of the day expects to be able to enjoy his children, eat supper and watch TV – and doesn't like the reality of tired babies, an exhausted partner looking to him for relief, a late meal and a disorganised house. (Occasionally, of course, it's the father who stays home but role reversal is still rare.)

Even today, mothers generally work longer hours than fathers. If they are in a job, their employment hours are shorter, but this is more than made up for by the hours they spend on child care and housework. A British survey found that over half of married women who were also in full-time jobs – and three-quarters of the women in a part-time job – did most or all of the housework. Where both partners are working full time, they are more likely to share the child care, but mothers who are not in employment are estimated to spend an average of fifty hours a week on child care alone.

This is where the idea of the 'Second Shift' comes in. Without ever thinking it through, many men feel that their working day ends when they leave the office or factory, and just assume that their partner's day ends when the children are asleep, the washing-up and ironing is done and the toys tidied away – several hours later. But a mother who has been looking after children from, say, seven in the morning until six in the evening when her partner gets home has already done a *longer* working day than he has. (And if he doesn't think looking after children full time is 'real work', perhaps he should try it for a day or two!)

In other words, the evening is a second shift for *both* of you. Once you both accept this, it's relatively easy to divide up what has to be done between you, whether on a regular basis or more casually. Some of the fathers we talked to prefer to take over both children's evening routine – bath, a late bottle and bedtime stories – while their partners organise supper and tidy up. Another couple divide the early evening between the two children; while the mother breastfeeds the baby and puts her to bed, father can spend time alone with the child. If the baby doesn't need a feed, he will spend time with her, allowing his partner to concentrate on the older child.

Depending on the children's bedtimes, sharing the work like this makes it possible on at least some evenings for you and your partner to get a bit of time together without the children – and that's vital too.

BEDTIME

It's important to try and organise a bedtime routine which suits you all. You may want to get both children into bed by, say, half past seven or eight to give yourselves time to catch up on what is left of the evening. Take advantage of the fact that while they're still young, this is usually manageable. By the time one or both children are at school, bedtime will be moving back to half past eight and later.

But if you and your partner are both in jobs, you may want to organise the evening differently. One couple who both have full-time jobs decided when their first baby was born to keep her up late (with a long daytime nap to compensate) so that they would have time with her after they came home from work at half past six or seven. Her younger brother now goes to bed at around eight, so that his parents have time with both children after they come home, while she continues to stay up until ten, giving her time alone with her parents.

In Britain, this is an extremely unusual arrangement – although in countries like Spain and Italy, it's very common to see children staying up late at night. As Martin commented:

> We sometimes envy parents who get their kids to bed early and can sit down and talk to each other over supper. We hardly ever manage that – although occasionally, we make sure our older child doesn't get an afternoon nap so that we can get her to bed before we eat. But generally we love our evenings with the children and we know that if we didn't keep them up late, we'd hardly see them at all during the week.

SPACE

However large or small your home, sharing out the space is important. Your first child has probably got used to having a room of her own and may resent having to share it with a newcomer.

If you have the room, you can avoid the problem by giving the second child a room of her own too. If your house is large enough, rearranging the rooms may help to solve the problem. Ann lives in a typical London terraced house, with a double living room on the ground floor and three bedrooms above.

> When I was expecting my third baby, I decided to reorganise the house. We turned the downstairs living room into two bedrooms for the two older children. The largest bedroom became the living room, leaving a bedroom each for me and the baby.

In most families, however, there's not much choice or you may prefer your children to share a room anyway. The big advantage of a shared room is that the children soon learn to entertain each other. Many parents have told us of the delight they feel early in the morning as they listen to the older child talking or 'reading' a story to a younger sister or brother – and a baby of only a few months old may be enchanted to be her audience.

Alison has experienced the advantages and disadvantages of both single and shared rooms with her three children.

> Dick was so foul to Tom that we could never let them share a room. So they each had their own room from when they were tiny. When Lucy arrived, we put her into Tom's room to share. To start with, Dick loved having his own room, being able to put his trains out all over the floor, and having a snug place of his own. But now he really feels quite sad at being excluded from Tom and Lucy's shared place, and he's always wanting to go in there to share a bedtime story.

A shared room helps to give each child some space of their own. It might be a special shelf or toy-box labelled with their name to keep particularly treasured possessions. They might each have a cupboard for their own clothes and toys, or a special individual quilt for their bed, or a noticeboard each for photos and pictures. Or each child could have their own things on the wall beside their bed.

In many shared bedrooms, there is only space for bunks. They can cause problems, however, if one child feels disadvantaged by having to sleep 'upstairs'. You might want to consider as an alternative installing two of the beds-on-platforms, where the bed is like the top of a bunk, with a desk and bookshelf built in underneath. That way, each child has a private space, and they don't have to sleep on top of each other. Obviously, this would only be suitable when both children are old enough to climb up to bed, and it is more expensive than bunks or two ordinary beds.

Just as you need to think about time for you and your partner, you also need to think about space for yourselves. Particularly as the children grow older and bicycles take over from manageably small 'sit 'n' rides', you may not want your children's activities and equipment taking over the entire house. You could, for instance, arrange your children's rooms as bed-and-playrooms, with only limited space for playing downstairs. Or you might decide to make over a basement or an attic conversion to your growing children. Obviously, the solution depends on your own house as well as what you need, but talking to your partner and your children about it might generate some fresh ideas.

CHILD CARE

If you and your partner are both in jobs, part time or full time, then you've already had to make child care arrangements for your first child. One advantage of having your children close together is that it can often be easier to extend your child care to include a second child. If they are both going to the same childminder – or if the childminder can collect the first child from school and look after both children until you get home – then the routine you've already established will not need to be dramatically changed.

Many working mothers in Britain rely on a grandmother or partner for child care, with childminders close behind. Indeed, some mothers decide to become childminders themselves when their children are young: if you do this, you should register with the social services department of the local authority. Nursery and crèche places for under-fives are still far too few.

What works for your first child, however, may not work for two. If you are relying on a grandmother, she may find taking on a baby as well as a toddler just too much – and some grandparents resent the way their daughter or daughter-in-law seem to take for granted their willingness to take care of the children. If you already have a good childminder, you'll obviously want to talk to her while you're pregnant about the possibility of her also taking the baby after you go back to work.

If there is a big age gap between your children, child care can impose real financial burdens, as Ann found:

> My older two are at school, so I haven't had to pay for full-time child care for several years. Now I've gone back to work after having a baby, I've had to start using a childminder again. Luckily she's able to

collect the older ones from school too, but it's costing me a very large part of what I earn. It'll be several years before Rebecca's at school too, and I can go back to just finding someone to care for them after school.

MONEY

It is easy to assume that a second child will be much cheaper than the first. After all, they can share the same equipment and pass on clothes. Unfortunately, it doesn't always work out like that!

Financially, it's a disadvantage to have two children very close in age. You may need two cots and two highchairs, as well as a double buggy. If you use a car, you'll need a second babyseat. If they're close in size as well as age, you may not even be able to pass down as many clothes as you expect. And whatever the age gap, you are going to need two beds and you will have to feed and equip two growing children.

There are some ways of cutting down on the cost. You may be able to persuade your older child to move into a bed before the baby is born (don't try and push her out of her cot afterwards to make way for the baby). If you think she'll only need the cot for a short time after the baby is born, you could use a carrycot or crib for the baby until the cot is free. Or you could try and borrow a second cot for a few months (ask the health visitor if she can help find one). If you have a travel cot, or can borrow or buy one second-hand, the baby can sleep very happily in that.

Handing down clothes helps, of course. Very small babies grow so fast that you probably have a drawer full of almost new baby clothes which will be inherited by your second child. If your children are the same sex, then handing down clothes is easier – although the younger child, as she grows older, may resent always wearing seconds. But if you have a boy and a girl, there's less scope for hand-me-downs. One mother we spoke to, who dressed her younger boy in his older sister's pink dungarees, was astonished by how many people were shocked by her failure to stick to blue.

One of the most expensive items of clothing – shoes – should never be handed down if you can possibly avoid it. With the exception of less fitted articles like wellington boots, slippers and trainers, second-hand shoes risk damaging a small child's growing feet.

TRANSPORT

One of the most difficult practical problems if you have two small children is getting them around. With your first, you probably had a buggy or a carrycot on wheels; or you may have splashed out on a big pram complete with hood. If your first child is old enough to walk everywhere, your baby can simply inherit whatever she had. But if your toddler still needs a lift at least some of the time, you need to find the best – and cheapest – way to add to your fleet.

While your baby is tiny, one of the easiest forms of transport is to combine a sling and a buggy. If you already have a sling from your first baby, you don't even

LIFE WITH TWO – THE PRACTICALITIES

have to invest in any new equipment. With the baby in the sling, you still have two (or one and a half!) hands free to push the toddler in the buggy, manage shopping, buy tickets and so on.

If you're taking both children on a bus or train, then this system means you only have a single buggy to fold up and stow away. When you're using public transport, it's easier to have the baby in a sling in front of you, so that the baby is against your chest; a baby back pack makes it almost impossible for you to sit down yourself. But if you're taking a longer walk, and don't need to use public transport, then a back pack can be more comfortable for you and give the baby a good view – while your toddler walks or is pushed. Many fabric slings are designed to be used either on your chest or your back and are, therefore, ideal while your baby is small. But if you do a lot of long walks, you may also need a sturdier back pack, with a proper frame, which gives both your baby and your back more support. When buying a back pack, do check that it meets proper safety standards (British Standards, or the equivalent European, American or Australian standard).

Extended use of a sling or back pack may keep you going until your toddler can walk everywhere and your baby can graduate to the buggy. But the age gap may be so small that you have to be able to push them together. If you already have a pram, you should be able to get a toddler seat designed to fit – provided that the pram is large and stable enough to carry two children. But do make sure it's securely fastened and fit a safety harness so that your child can't fall out.

DOUBLE BUGGIES

Sooner or later, you will probably have to face the double buggy. It *ought* to be easy to get a double buggy which:

- goes through your front door *and* the door and turnstile of your local supermarket

- is easy to fold and light to carry
- has space for your shopping
- is strong enough to last

A double buggy might see your first two children through until the first is, say, four, and then have to cope with a third baby and second child.

In fact, it's almost impossible.

Here are some points to consider before you buy. (We've referred to specific manufacturers as a guide, but because models and prices change quickly it makes sense to shop around.)

WIDTH

The first problem is that if a double buggy is wide enough to seat two children comfortably, then it's probably too wide to go through your front door – and may be awkward in the shops. If it's narrow enough to go through doors easily, the children may be rather squashed. (A buggy with one wide seat, designed for twins, may be fine when your second child is tiny, but won't have enough room for a toddler and a growing baby.)

Before you buy, measure your own front door (84 cm is the normal width). If you use a particular shop or supermarket regularly, it's worth measuring there as well: you may get some funny looks, but it's better than getting stuck in the door every time you visit! Unfortunately, most supermarkets have turnstile entrances which no double buggy goes through: you'll need to ask to be let through, or go elsewhere. (It's always worth pointing out to the management that they simply don't cater for parents with children. If enough people do this, they may finally change their layout.)

CARRYCOT, SEATS OR BOTH?

If you're planning to use a double buggy from the day your baby is born, you may want one which will take a carrycot as an alternative to one of the seats. Some double buggies allow one or both seats to recline flat, so that they will take a tiny baby. But you need to make sure that the baby will be warm enough, which means a padded seat and/or a buggy 'apron' (the woollen envelope which covers the baby from her toes right up to her chest) as well as a rainhood.

Mama's and Papa's and Cosmos make double buggies with seats that will go flat enough to take a baby. Mothercare, Maclaren, Bebecar and Cindico all make double buggies which will take one or two carrycots in place of the seats.

SHOPPING

If you're used to a single buggy with a shopping tray underneath, then it can be a real nuisance to find yourself with a double buggy with no space for your bags. You may end up hanging shopping bags on the handle of the buggy – with the risk, of course, that the buggy falls over backwards as soon as one child gets out.

Both Mama's and Papa's and Cosmos make double buggies with their own shopping trays. Double check that you can fold the buggy with the shopping tray attached. (You should also be able to fold it with the rainhood in place.)

TANDEM BUGGIES

There is an alternative to the double buggy, more often seen in other European countries than in Britain. This is the 'tandem' buggy where the children sit *behind* each other instead of side by side. They are more expensive than most double buggies, but they are narrow enough to go through almost any doorway – and, in some versions, they will take three or even four babies. So they're the perfect solution if you have three children very close in age, or twins with a sibling, or triplets.

The manufacturers to look for are Petrena, who make 'Triplet' (two seats behind, one in front) and 'Quad' (two behind two), and Emmaljunga, who make 'Duette' (one behind the other) and 'Baby Bus' (with a raised seat behind, complete with footrest on which a toddler can sit, and a baby seat in front).

The length of these tandem buggies can be a problem. If you want to fold it and take it in your car, you should check that it will fit. And you may not be able to take it in smaller lifts.

TRAVELLING IN CARS

With only one baby, you can choose between a baby car seat and installing straps to hold a carrycot safely on the back seat. With a baby and an older child, or two babies, you are more restricted. Because a carrycot takes up the middle part of the back seat, it's difficult to combine with a seat for an older child.

The most versatile option is to choose one of the newer car seats which can be used in the *front* seat, facing backwards, while the baby is still very small, and then be switched to the back seat, facing forwards, when he is bigger. Your first child can start in one of these, then move to a bigger child seat before moving on to a booster seat. The second baby can start using the baby seat as soon as you are ready to take him out, and then move up later into the child seat.

One of the advantages of this system is that your two children don't have to sit next to each other until they're both older! It is almost impossible for a driver to cope with two fighting children – or an older child attacking a baby – in the seat behind you. This way, you have your baby in the passenger seat beside you, and your child behind you, able to see and to talk to you but safely out of reach of the baby! Any additional adults can go in the back seat and help entertain the toddler.

When you're buying a baby seat, check:

- British Standard approval, or the equivalent European, North American or Australasian standard. In Britain, there are special safety standards to which baby seats must conform, and it is illegal to carry a baby in the front seat on a car *except* in an approved, rear-facing baby seat.

- That it will fit your safety belts. Baby seats designed for use in the front seat of a car generally say that they will fit any make. But one family we talked to found that their Volvo's specially designed safety belts were too short to fit properly around a rear-facing seat. The Volvo system – carrycot restraint on the back seat followed by a child seat – doesn't cope with two small children (or twins).
- That it is sturdy enough for your needs. If you are buying a baby seat for your first baby, and want it to last for your second and even a third child, then you need to look for one of the heavier models with a metal frame. Several parents have told us that the plastic frames of the original, lightweight rear-facing baby seats simply collapsed after about two years' wear. But if you only want the seat to last for one baby, a lighter model (preferably with a carrying handle) should be fine.

If you need to be able to transport your children in other people's cars – a childminder's or grandparent's, for instance – then you will also need the kind of car seat that is held by seat belts, rather than one which requires its own special fittings.

Because rear-facing baby seats have been around for several years now, you may be able to buy one second-hand. Check that the safety harness is in good condition and that the joints of the frame are solid. Your antenatal clinic is likely to be a good source of information about second-hand equipment.

SAFE BEHAVIOUR IN CARS

With more than one child, the issue of safe behaviour in the car becomes vital. Children fighting in the back seat distract the driver and can be extremely dangerous. Mandy found that the only way to deal with the problem was to turn the car into a 'home on wheels':

> We kept a large bag of games in the car permanently, so that there was always something for the children to play with. We never went on a long journey without an adequate supply of drink and food.

Provided your children don't get carsick, books and puzzles may be a useful distraction; if they do suffer from carsickness, then you have to allow for regular stops as well.

It makes sense to have a very firm rule that no fighting is allowed in the car. If the children do start fighting, the driver should stop and refuse to move off again until the fight stops. You may also be able to put a bit of space between the children, by putting each child at one end of the rear passenger seat and asking any extra adult passenger to sit between them.

Some parents find it easier to tackle long journeys at night, getting children into pyjamas and ready for sleep before they set off. Whatever solution you find for your family, time spent in preparing for a car journey with children is never wasted!

TRAVELLING BY PLANE

Taking two or three children on a plane can be daunting, especially if you're the only adult. Most airlines, however, help by allowing you to push your buggy right up to the plane and collect it again when you get off. On a very long journey, phone the airline in advance to ask for an 'escort' to help you and the children get from the check-in to the plane. And check what the airline provides: Qantas and British Airways, for instance, stock ample nappies, milk and juice, so that you only need to carry enough supplies for stop-overs.

SAFETY AT HOME

Thousands of children every year are injured in their own home – some of them fatally. When your first child was born, you probably took several safety precautions like installing a guard on the fireplace and gates on the staircase and blocking off electric sockets. But as one child grows older, it is easy to forget the precautions which are needed for a new baby.

The answer is to start again with your new baby. Go round your home checking for danger points as if this was the first time you'd done it. If you don't already have a home safety checklist, you should be able to get one from your health visitor. The key points to check are:

- Electric sockets – any socket which could be reached by a baby or child should be protected by a safety plug.
- Stairs – if your first child has outgrown the need for safety gates, you'll need to get them out again when your baby starts crawling.
- Fireplaces *must* be protected by a nursery guard.
- Cooking hobs should be protected by a safety rail. And never leave a saucepan with the handle projecting over the edge – a toddler could reach up and tip it over.
- Hot drinks and kettles. When you're holding your baby in your arms, *never* leave your cup of tea near the edge of the table where she can reach out and grab it.
- Baths – if you haven't already got a non-slip rubber mat, it's a good idea to get one now. And of course, never leave a young child unattended in the bath, even for a minute. If you have to answer the doorbell or phone, take the child with you – even if you do get wet!
- Trailing wires – if it moves, the baby will grab it! Check whether your baby might pull a telephone down on to her head, and try to keep television leads out of reach.

While your baby is still young, a playpen provides a safe place. But don't assume that a baby in a playpen is safe from a jealous older sister or brother: if you have any fear that your toddler may hurt the baby, then the only safe rule is never to leave them alone together. But we hope that this book will have helped you to help your children get on so well that such drastic measures will no longer be needed.

Appendix I Your rights at work

This Appendix provides a summary of your rights to:
- Time off for antenatal care.
- Change your work while pregnant.
- Protection against dismissal because of pregnancy.
- Return to your job after maternity leave.
- Paid maternity leave.

ANTENATAL CARE

You are entitled to paid time off work for antenatal care, including time needed to travel to your clinic or GP. 'Antenatal' care includes relaxation classes and sessions about preparation for labour, as well as the actual appointments with your doctor or midwife.

This applies from the first day you start working for your employer. It doesn't matter how many hours you work.

Let your employer know when you need time off and how long you are likely to be absent. After the first appointment, your employer can ask to see your appointment card and a certificate signed by your GP, midwife or health visitor, confirming that you are pregnant.

IF YOUR WORK IS DANGEROUS

If the work that you do while you are pregnant is dangerous or illegal (for instance, working with certain chemicals or with X-rays), then you may be entitled to move to another job with the same employer, if one is available.

This only applies if you have been with the employer for two years if you work for sixteen hours or more a week, or five years if you work between eight and sixteen hours a week. (If you work under eight hours a week, you do not qualify at all.)

If there is another job for you to do, then you are still entitled to the same terms and conditions of employment as you have in your present job. If there is no suitable alternative at all, you can be fairly dismissed – but you still keep your rights to paid maternity leave.

DISMISSAL BECAUSE OF PREGNANCY

It is unlawful for your employer to dismiss you because you are pregnant – provided you have worked there for at least two years (between sixteen hours or more a week) or for five years, if you work between eight and sixteen hours a week.

If you haven't been with your employers long enough, you may still be covered by the Sex Discrimination Act. The Equal Opportunities Commission, Overseas House, Quay Street, Manchester M3 3HN, can provide further information.

MATERNITY LEAVE

You may be entitled to return to your own job (or a similar one) for up to twenty-nine weeks after the baby is born.

While you are pregnant, you may not know whether you will want to return to work or whether you will be able to get adequate child care once you have another child. It makes sense to *keep your options open* by saying that you intend to return to work in advance. You can always change your mind later.

If, however, your firm employs five or fewer people, they can refuse to take you back if it is 'not reasonably practicable to do so'. If you and your boss disagree about whether or not it's possible for you to have your job back, you can ask an industrial tribunal to decide.

In order to qualify for your job back, you must:

1. Have worked for the same employers continuously for at least two years by the end of the twelfth week before the week the baby is due. (Two years applies if you work sixteen or more hours a week; if you work between eight and sixteen hours a week, you have to have been there for at least five years.)
2. Work at least until the end of the twelfth week before the baby is due. (Being absent because of sickness or holiday doesn't count against you.) To work out the dates, find the Sunday immediately before the day your baby is due and count back eleven Sundays; you have to work up until the Friday before that Sunday (or the Saturday if you normally work Saturdays).
3. Write to your employers at least twenty-one days before you go on leave, saying that you will be taking maternity leave *and* intend to return to work. The employers are entitled to have a copy of the maternity certificate which you can get from your midwife or GP.
4. Write to your employers again at least twenty-one days before you actually return to work.

Your employers are also entitled to write to you, starting from seven weeks after your baby is born, asking if you still plan to return to work. You *must* reply in writing within fourteen days to keep your right to return!

RETURNING PART TIME

You don't have a legal right to return to work part time if you were previously employed full time. (In Sweden, by contrast, parents of young children have the right to reduce their working day from eight to six hours if they choose.)

You can, of course, ask to reduce your hours of work after your baby is born. It is up to your employer whether or not to agree. If you are in a trade union, you should ask for their help. If your employer does agree, you should ask for 'continuity of employment' so that your part-time job isn't treated as *new* employment with the company. If you allow your old contract of employment to be ended, then you will have to start all over again building up the two years' service (or five years if you are now working between eight and sixteen hours a week) before you can qualify again for maternity leave or certain other legal rights.

DELAYING YOUR RETURN TO WORK

Normally, your right to go back to your job only applies for up to twenty-nine weeks after your baby is born. If you are ill, however, you can delay your return for up to another four weeks. But you must let your employers know of the delay *before* the date when they expected you to return, and you must send in a medical certificate.

Your employers can also delay your return for up to four weeks, but must tell you why and give you a new date for your return.

TAKING TWO MATERNITY LEAVES

You may already have taken one lot of maternity leave and gone back to your old job after having your first baby. In that case, there should be no problem about qualifying again for maternity leave, even if your two babies are born very close together.

Carol had worked for her firm as a repairs engineer for nearly two years when she became pregnant with her first baby. So she was able to qualify for maternity leave because she had worked for more than two years by twelve weeks before his expected date of birth. She stopped work two months before the baby was due, and went back to the same job four months (seventeen weeks) after he was born. Three months later, she found she was pregnant again. By the time she got to twelve weeks before the second baby's expected birthday, she had worked for the firm for three and a half years (including the first maternity leave). So even though she had only been back at work for about six months after her first maternity leave, she still qualified for a second maternity leave.

The important point is that you must have 'continuous employment' with the same employer in order to link the two periods before and after your first maternity leave. Provided you return to work within twenty-nine weeks of your first baby's birth, this should not pose any problem.

A difficulty could arise, however, if you changed from full-time to part-time work after your first baby was born, even though you return to your old firm. If possible, as we explain above, you should get your employer to agree that you will keep your 'continuity of employment' so that the years during which you worked full time are added to the time you work part time in calculating future entitlement to maternity leave.

Your employer may also have a more generous maternity leave scheme than the twenty-nine weeks provided by law. Some companies, for instance, allow people to return to their old job up to one year after the baby's birth. Again, provided you return within the period allowed by your employer, you will be entitled to take maternity leave again with your second baby.

If, however, you started with a new employer after your first baby was born, then you will have to qualify again for a second maternity leave. If you are working sixteen hours or more a week, this means working at least two years up until the end of the twelfth week before the baby is due. If you are working between eight and sixteen hours a week, you will need to stay for at least five years before you qualify for maternity leave.

MATERNITY PAY

You may be entitled to Statutory Maternity Pay (SMP) for up to eighteen weeks of your maternity leave.

You qualify for the basic rate of SMP if:

- You have worked for your employer for at least six months by the end of the *fifteenth* week before your baby is due.
- You are still employed in this fifteenth week.
- You earn at least £43 a week on average.

In 1989, the basic rate of SMP was £36.25 a week.

APPENDIX I – YOUR RIGHTS AT WORK

You qualify for the higher rate of SMP if:

You have worked for your employer for at least two years (sixteen hours a week or more) by the end of the fifteenth week before the baby is due (or five years if you work between eight and sixteen hours a week).

The higher rate of SMP is nine-tenths of your average pay. It is only paid for the first six weeks.

SMP lasts for up to eighteen weeks (six weeks at the higher rate, if you qualify, the rest at the basic rate). You cannot start getting it until you go on maternity leave. It can then be paid for any eighteen-week period between the eleventh week before your baby is due and eleven weeks after the baby is born.

You can start your maternity leave eleven weeks before the baby is due, and draw SMP immediately. In that case (provided your baby is born on the expected date) your SMP will last until the baby is seven weeks old.

You may, however, want to work until nearer the date of birth. Because SMP stops when the baby is eleven weeks old, it makes sense to stop work at least seven weeks before the baby is due. Otherwise, you will lose one week's SMP for each week that you go on working.

To get SMP, write to your employer at least three weeks before you stop work, asking for your SMP and sending them a copy of your maternity certificate, which you get from your midwife or GP. If you haven't got your maternity certificate, *write anyway*. You can always send the certificate later, but you may lose your SMP if you don't give three weeks' notice.

Your employers should pay your SMP in the same way as your wages, deducting any tax and National Insurance contributions.

Your employer may, of course, have a more generous scheme for paid maternity leave. Some companies provide three months on full pay; others offer three months on full pay followed by three months' half pay. If you are planning another baby, or in the early stages of pregnancy, and your employer doesn't have a maternity leave scheme, it is worth asking – or getting your trade union to ask for you.

MATERNITY ALLOWANCE

If you don't qualify for SMP – because you are self-employed or because you changed jobs while pregnant, for instance – you may qualify for maternity allowance.

To get maternity allowance you must have paid full national insurance contributions for at least twenty-six of the fifty-two weeks ending with the fifteenth week before the baby is due.

Maternity allowance in 1989 was £33.20 a week. Like SMP, it can be paid for up to eighteen weeks.

If you don't know whether or not you qualify, *claim anyway*. You claim on form MA1 which you should be able to get from your antenatal clinic or social security office. You will also need your maternity certificate from your GP or midwife. Send your claim form, and the certificate, to your local social security office – and make the claim as soon as possible after you are twenty-six weeks pregnant.

SOCIAL FUND MATERNITY PAYMENT

New parents used to receive an automatic maternity grant of £25. That has been abolished and replaced by payments from the Social Fund which only go to parents on low incomes who are receiving certain benefits.

If you are receiving income support or family credit, you can claim a lump sum payment from the Social Fund to help buy things for your new baby. The payment is £85 for each baby. If you have more than £585 in savings, you cannot get the payment; if your savings are between £500 and £585, the payment will be reduced.

You can claim the maternity payment on form SF100 from the social security office. Again, you need to send in your maternity certificate as well. If you are claiming after your baby's birth, send a copy of the baby's birth certificate instead. You can claim up to three months after your baby is born.

Appendix II Useful organisations

The organisations listed below are a selection of the many which are relevant to the various needs of parents and children. Some have local branches, while others have only a national office or coordinator. Most are run on very low budgets and the majority rely on unpaid voluntary labour. So please be patient when you are contacting them – you may not receive an immediate reply, and the telephones might be staffed for only a few hours a day.

When writing, please enclose a large (10" × 7") stamped addressed envelope to help with the relevant organisation's mailing costs which are very high these days. Remember also that the offices of associations tend to change quite frequently and an address published here may go out of date quite quickly.

It's usually worth consulting local sources of help to see if a group has been set up in your area. Your Yellow Pages telephone directory is one possibility and your GP or health visitor will also probably know of local support or self-help groups. Public libraries are a good source of information (ask the librarian), and your branch will probably have a current copy of *The Voluntary Agencies Directory*, published by the National Council for Voluntary Organisations, 26 Bedford Square, London WC1B 3HU which lists around 2,000 voluntary groups. Your local Citizens' Advice Bureau is likely to have details of most local groups, too.

Most towns and rural areas have a local voluntary service council which coordinates the activities of such groups and keeps an up-to-date list of them. You can contact yours by checking one of the above sources of help, if you don't already know its whereabouts.

List of Organisations

Active Birth Centre
55 Dartmouth Park Road, London NW5 1SL.
Telephone 01 267 3006.
Offers education, advice and special classes for women wanting natural childbirth. Special emphasis on yoga, relaxation, exercises and water birth.

Advisory Centre for Education
18 Victoria Park Square, London E2 9PB.
Telephone 01 980 4596.
Campaigns for improvements in state education and has advisory service for parents of children in state schools.

Association of Breastfeeding Mothers
10 Herschel Road, London SE23 1EG.
Telephone 01 778 4769.
Has local branches and network of counsellors to support women who are breastfeeding.

Association for Improvements in Maternity Services
40 Kingswood Avenue, London NW6 6LS.
Telephone 01 278 5628.
Offers information, support and advice on all aspects of maternity care and campaigns for parents rights in pregnancy and childbirth.

Association for Postnatal Illness
7 Gowan Avenue, London SW6 6RH.
Telephone 01 731 4867.
Offers advice and support for women suffering from postnatal depression and has a network of volunteer supporters.

British Association for Counselling
37a Sheep Street, Rugby, Warwickshire CV21 3BX.
Telephone 0788 78328/9.
Maintains an up-to-date list of counsellors and psychotherapists all over the country.

BLISS (Baby Life Support Systems)
17–21 Emerald Street, London WC1N 3QL.
Telephone 01 831 9393/8996.
Campaigns for more equipment for intensive and special care units for sick and premature babies. Also has *Blisslink*, a support service for parents of sick and premature babies.

British Association of Psychotherapists
121 Hendon Lane, London N3 3PR.
Telephone 01 346 1747.
Members offer psychotherapy for adults and children along analytic lines.

British Institute for Brain-Injured Children
Knowle Hall, Knowle, Bridgewater, Somerset TA7 8PJ.
Telephone 0278 684060.
Offers assessment and treatment for children who are brain damaged.

Caesarean Support Network
2 Hurst Park Drive, Huyton, Liverpool L36 1TF.
Offers information, support and advice to women who are about to, or have undergone a Caesarean section.

Children Need Fathers
18 Green Lane, Grendon Atherstone, Warwickshire CV9 2PL.
Telephone 08277 4389.
Campaigns for the rights of fathers and their role in the family, especially in divorce and separation.

Childwatch
60 Beck Road, Everthorpe, South Cave, North Humberside HU15 2JJ.
Telephone 04302 3824 or 0482 25552.
Campaigns in connection with family violence and child abuse and for better public education in these matters.

Compassionate Friends
6 Denmark Street, Bristol BS1 5DQ.
Telephone 0272 292778.
Offers support and friendship to bereaved parents who have lost a child.

Contact a Family
16 Strutton Ground, London SW1P 2HP.
Telephone 01 222 2695.
Offers information, advice and support for parents of children with all kinds of handicaps.

Cry-sis, BM Cry-sis Support Group
London WC1N 3XX.
Telephone 01 404 5011.
Offers a support and information service for parents of young children with crying or sleeping problems. Has local coordinators of branches.

Children's Cancer Help Centre
PO Box 4, Orpington, Kent BR6 8Q7.
Telephone 0689 71587.
Offers support and advice for families with a child suffering from cancer.

Cleft Lip and Palate Association (CLAPA)
1 Eastwood Gardens, Kenton, Newcastle-upon-Tyne, NE3 3DQ.
Telephone 091 285 9396.
Offers counselling, support and information to parents of infants born with this kind of abnormality.

Down's Syndrome Association
12–13 Clapham Common Southside, London SW4 7AA.
Telephone 01 720 0008.

APPENDIX II – USEFUL ORGANISATIONS

Parents' self-help organisation to support families where there is a child (young or grown up) suffering from Down's syndrome.

End Physical Punishment of Children (EPOCH)
77 Holloway Road, London N7 8JZ.
Telephone 01 700 0627.
Campaigns to bring an end to all forms of physical punishment to children by parents and all other adults.

Exploring Parenthood Trust
Omnibus Workspace 41 North Road, London N7 9DP.
Telephone 01 700 4822.
Runs workshops and support groups for parents of children of all ages and social backgrounds under professional guidance.

Families Need Fathers
BM Families, London WC1N 3XX.
Telephone 01 852 7123.
Gives support and help to both fathers and mothers following separation or divorce and advice on access or custody problems.

Family Planning Association
27–35 Mortimer Street, London W1N 7RJ.
Telephone 01 636 7866.
Education, advice and medical service for individuals and couples concerning all aspects of contraception, family planning and sexual/emotional relationships. Also runs mail order book service.

Food and Chemical Allergy Association
27 Ferringham Lane, Ferring-by-Sea, West Sussex BN12 5NB.
Telephone 0903 41178.
Offers help and information about food and chemical allergies.

Foresight (Association for the Promotion of Preconceptual Care)
The Old Vicarage, Church Lane, Witley, Godalming, Surrey GU8 5PN.
Telephone 0428 794500.
Offers advice and information for parents to promote optimal health before conception and during pregnancy, with a special emphasis on nutrition and avoidance of environmental hazards.

Foundation for the Study of Infant Deaths
15 Belgrave Square, London SW1X 8PS.
Telephone 01 235 0965 or answering machine on 01 235 1721.
Promotes research into cot death and related illnesses in young babies and offers support for bereaved parents.

Gifted Children's Information Centre
Hampton Grange, 21 Hampton Lane, Solihull B91 2QJ.
Telephone 021 7054547.
Offers free telephone counselling to parents and arranges assessment of gifted and dyslexic children and others with handicaps.

Gingerbread
35 Wellington Street, London WC2E 7BN.
Telephone 01 240 0953.
Provides support, information, local groups and practical help for lone parents, as well as social activities and holiday schemes.

Hyperactive Children's Support Group
71 Whyke Lane, Chichester, Sussex.
Telephone 0903 725182.
Offers help and support for hyperactive children and their families plus ideas for overcoming this kind of problem, especially using dietary information.

Holiday Endeavour for Lone Parents
52 Chequer Avenue, Hyde Park, Doncaster DN4 5AS.
Telephone 0302 65139.
Seeks to provide low cost holidays for single parent families in Britain.

Home and School Council
81 Rustlings Road, Sheffield S11 7AB.
Telephone 0742 662467.
Disseminates information on aspects of home and school relations and coordinates parents' education organisations.

Kidscape
82 Brook Street, London W1Y 1YG.
Telephone 01 493 9845.
Education, information and advice service to help prevent all kinds of danger and abuse of children.

La Lèche League of Great Britain
PO Box BM3424, London WC1N 3XX.
Telephone 01 242 1278 or 01 504 5011.
Offers support and counselling for breastfeeding mothers, with local groups and a 24-hour telephone counselling service.

Maternity Alliance
15 Britannia Street, London WC1X 9JP.
Telephone 01 837 1265.
Offers a support and information service about maternity rights and benefits and campaigns on maternity issues.

Miscarriage Association
18 Stonybrook Close, West Bretton, Wakefield, West Yorkshire WF4 4TP.
Telephone 0924 85515.
Offers information and support for women who have had a miscarriage.

Meet-a-Mum Association (MAMA)
5 Westbury Gardens, Luton, Bedfordshire LU2 7DW.
Telephone 0582 422253.
National support group with local branches for mothers of young children and especially those suffering from postnatal depression.

Mothers Apart from Their Children (MATCH)
c/o BM Problems, London WC1N 3XX.
Telephone 01 404 5011.
Offers support and help for mothers who are separated from their children for whatever reason.

National Association For Gifted Children
1 South Audley Street, London W1Y 5DQ.
Telephone 01 499 1188.
Runs a voluntary counselling service for parents of gifted children. Local branches offer activities for youngsters of all ages.

National Association for the Welfare of Children in Hospital (NAWCH)
Argyle House, 29–31 Euston Road, London NW1 2SD.
Telephone 01 833 2041.
Campaigns on behalf of parents whose children go into hospital to ensure better facilities and planning for them. Offers an information and advice service for parents. Also has local branches.

National Childbirth Trust
Alexandra House, Oldham Terrace, Acton, London W3 6NH.
Telephone 01 992 8637.
Has a national network of local branches that offer classes in natural childbirth, postnatal support and breastfeeding counselling.

National Childcare Campaign Ltd
Wesley House, 4 Wild Court, London WC2B 5AU.
Telephone 01 405 5617.
Campaigns for free nurseries and properly organised child care facilities for the under-fives. Has an information service for parents.

National Childminding Association
8 Masons Hill, Bromley BR2 9EY.
Telephone 01 464 6164.
Primarily to coordinate and further the training and status of childminders and to improve links between parents and minders.

National Council for the Divorced and Separated
13 High Street, Little Shelford, Cambridgeshire CB2 5ES.
Telephone 021 588 5757.
Has local branches and a counselling service for people affected by divorce or separation.

National Council for One Parent Families
255 Kentish Town Road, London NW5 2LX.

APPENDIX II – USEFUL ORGANISATIONS

Telephone 01 267 1361.
Offers help and advice for single parents on any problem and campaigns on behalf of them and their children for better facilities and support.

National Eczema Society
Tavistock House North, Tavistock Square, London WC1H 9SR.
Telephone 01 388 4097.
Offers information and support for eczema sufferers and their families and raises funds for research into this condition.

National Family Conciliation Council
34 Milton Road, Swindon, Wiltshire SN1 5JA.
Telephone 0793 618486.
Fosters the provision of conciliation services for parents who have difficulty agreeing over arrangements for children in divorce and separation.

National Information for Parents of Prematures: Education, Resources and Support (NIPPERS)
c/o The Sam Segal Perinatal Unit, St Mary's Hospital, Praed Street, London W2 1NY.
Telephone 01 992 9301.
Support and advice for parents of premature and sick babies through hospital special-care units and parent-to-parent contact.

Parentline-OPUS
106 Goldstone Road, Whyteleafe, Surrey CR3 06B.
Telephone 01 645 0469 (administration) or 01 645 0505 (24-hour enquiry service).
This was set up to prevent child abuse and to help and support parents under stress, with local branches and a telephone counselling service.

The Parent Network
44–46 Caversham Road, London NW5 2DS.
Telephone 01 485 8535.
Set up to establish a national network of support groups for parents, run by parents. Aims to improve relationships and communication in families.

Parents Anonymous
6–7 Manor Gardens, London N7 6LA.
Telephone 01 236 8918 (24-hour answering service).
Offers support and a telephone counselling service for parents under stress and at risk of abusing their children.

Play for Life
31B Ipswich Road, Norwich NR2 2LN.
Telephone 0603 505947.
Promotes the development of play through life affirming toys and cooperative games and activities, rather than competitive or warlike ones. Has a mail order catalogue.

Practical Alternatives for Mums, Dads and Under-Fives (PRAM)
c/o 162 Holland Road, Hurst Green, Oxted, Surrey RH8 9BQ.
Set up to promote facilities for young families and to publicise information about local facilities.

Pre-Eclamptic Toxaemia Society (PETS)
Ty Iago, High Street, Llanberis, Caernarvon, Gwynedd LL55 4HB.
Telephone 0286 872477.
Offers help and support to women who have suffered from pre-eclamptic toxaemia and advice about ways of preventing the illness.

Pre-School Playgroups Association
National Centre, 61–63 King's Cross Road, London WC1N 9LL.
Telepone 01 833 0991.
Promotes and provides a variety of playgroup facilities where parents can be involved in the pre-school development of their under-fives.

Relate
Herbert Gray College, Little Church Street, Rugby, Warwickshire CV21 3AP.
Telephone 0788 73241.

Formerly known as the National Marriage Guidance Council, it offers counselling for anyone experiencing problems in their relationship, alone or with a partner. Details of local branches from the head office above or from your telephone directory.

Relaxation for Living
29 Burwood Park Road, Walton-on-Thames, Surrey KT12 5LH.
Promotes relaxation and health through learning how to handle stress, with classes, books and tapes.

Society to Support Home Confinements
Lydgate, Lydgate Lane, Wolsingham, Bishop Auckland, Co Durham DL13 3HA.
Telephone 09565 528044.
Offers support and advice for women wanting to give birth at home, especially those who are meeting obstacles.

Stepfamily
162 Tenison Road, Cambridge CB1 2DP.
Telephone 0223 460312.
Offers advice, counselling and information for people living in stepfamilies. Covers all aspects ranging from practical to emotional.

Stillbirth and Neonatal Death Society (SANDS)
28 Portland Place, London W1N 4DE.
Telephone 01 436 5881.
Offers information, support and counselling for parents who lose a baby through stillbirth or neonatal death.

Twins and Multiple Births Association (TAMBA)
41 Fortuna Way, Aylesby Park, Grimsby, South Humberside DN37 9SJ
Telephone 0472 883182.
Offers support and encouragement for parents of twins, triplets and so on, as well as a network of local groups.

We Welcome Small Children Campaign
93a Belsize Lane, London NW3 5AY.
Telephone 01 586 3453.
Campaigns for better facilities for families with young children in towns and shopping centres and so on. Publicises these facilities and coordinates local activities in other areas.

Working Mothers Association
77 Holloway Road, London N7 8JZ.
Telephone 01 700 5771.
This is a self-help organisation set up to support working mothers and their children with information and advice as well as local groups.

Australia

For advice on the existing laws regarding women's rights at work

Women's Bureau
Department of Employment and Industrial Relations
PO Box 9880
Canberra ACT 2601
Tel: (062) 459 111

For advice or complaints against the infringements of rights

Anti-Discrimination Board
Level II
Legal & General Building
8–18 Bent Street
Sydney NSW 2000
Tel: (02) 224 8200

Human Rights & Equal Opportunity Commission
Level 2A
American Express Building
388 George Street
Sydney NSW 2000
Tel: (02) 229 7600
(The Sex Discrimination Act 1984 is designed to promote equality of men and women and to eliminate discrimination on the basis of sex, marital status or pregnancy. The Act covers discrimination in employment, education, accommodation and the provision of goods and services. Complaints

APPENDIX II – USEFUL ORGANISATIONS

under the Act are accepted by the Commission and its agencies in other States.)

The Family Planning Association in Australia.
Services include: birth control, pregnancy testing & counselling; sex education; advice and referral service for women. It has an extensive library and resource centre which is open to the public.

FPA/ACT
Health Promotion Centre
Childers Street
Canberra ACT 2601
Tel: (062) 47 3077

FPA/NSW
161 Broadway
Broadway NSW 2007
Tel: (02) 211 0244

FPA/NT
Shop 11
Rapid Creek Shopping Centre
Trower Road
Rapid Creek NT 0810
Tel: (089) 480 144

FPA/QLD
100 Alfred Street
Fortitude Valley QLD 4006
Tel: (07) 252 5151

FPA/SA
17 Phillips Street
Kensington SA 5068
Tel: (08) 31 5177

Family Planning Tasmania
73 Federal Street
North Hobart TAS 7002
Tel: (002) 34 7790

FPA/VIC
266/272 Church Street
Richmond VIC 3121
Tel: (03) 429 3500

FPA/WA
70 Roe Street
(Cnr Roe and Lake Streets)
Northbridge WA 6000
Tel: (09) 227 6177

Portfolio Issues Unit
Department of Industrial Relations
GPO Box 9879
Canberra ACT 2601
Tel: (062) 437333
Provides advice and action on industrial matters.

Office of the Status of Women
Department of the Prime Minister and Cabinet
3–5 National Circuit
Barton ACT 2600
Tel: (062) 715722
Provides policy advice to the Prime Minister and the Minister responsible for the status of women and child care issues.

Working Womens Centre
49–51 Flinders Street
Liverpool Building
Adelaide SA 5000
Tel: (08) 2240188
Handles queries regarding all aspects of women's employment.

Child Care Administration and Development Branch
Department of Community Services and Health
GPO Box 9848
Canberra ACT 2601
Tel: 891555
(Same address for **Child Care and Strategic Planning Branch**)
Provides policy advice to Commonwealth government on child care issues.

Affirmative Action Agency
1st Floor
65 Berry Street
North Sydney NSW 2060
Tel: (02) 9634904
Administers Affirmative Action Act 1986

Canada

Prenatal and Parenthood Education Services Metropolitan Toronto
3089 Bathurst Street
Suite 319
Toronto M6A 2A4
Tel: 787 1259

Planned Parenthood of Toronto
36B Prince Arthur Avenue
Toronto M5R 1A9
Tel: 961 0113

Ontario Ministry of Labour Employment Standards Branch
400 University Avenue
3rd Floor
Toronto M7A 1V2
Tel: 965 5251

Canadian Mothercraft Society
32 Heath Street West
Toronto M4V 1T3
Tel: 920 3515

Canada Employment and Immigration Commission
Employment and Insurance Division
55 St Clair Avenue East
7th Floor
Toronto M4T 1M2
Tel: 730 1211
(The Unemployment Insurance Act covers most employed persons who have an interruption of earnings due to shortage of work, illness, injury, pregnancy or adoption. It also provides benefits to fathers who become the primary caregivers to a newborn child.)

Bibliography

Bank, Stephen, P., and Kahn, Michael, D., *The Sibling Bond*, Basic Books, NY, 1982
Biddulph, Steve, *The Secret of Happy Families*, Bay Books, Australia, 1985
Brandt, Herbert, *Childbirth for Men*, OUP, 1985
Corkille Briggs, Dorothy, *Your Child's Self-Esteem*, Dolphin Books, Doubleday & Co Inc, NY, 1975
Daws, Dilys, *Through the Night: Helping Parents and Sleepless Infants*, Free Association Books, 1989
Dunn, Judy, and Kendrick, Carol, *Siblings: Love, Envy and Understanding*, Grant McIntyre, 1982
Kitzinger, Sheila, *Freedom and Choice in Childbirth*, Penguin, 1988
Kitzinger, Sheila, *Giving Birth: How It Really Feels*, Victor Gollancz, 1987
Leach, Penelope, *Baby and Child*, Michael Joseph, 1988
Newson, John, and Newson, Elizabeth, *The Extent of Parental Physical Punishment in the UK*, The Association for the Protection of All Children Ltd, 1989
Parke, Ross D., *Fathering*, Fontana, 1981

Index

abnormality *see* disability
abortion 10, 22–4
accidental pregnancy 6, 10–13
age gap 13–16
   advantages and disadvantages 16
   financial considerations 108
   and jealousy 14, 50
aeroplane, travel by 113
aggression 53, 80
allowance, maternity 117
amniocentesis 22–4
anaemia 15, 16, 21
anger 53, 76–9
antenatal checks 26, 114
Association of Breastfeeding Mothers 42, 119
attacks on mother 54–7
Australia, addresses 124
authoritarian approach 71, 73

baby blues 45–7 *see also* postnatal depression
babysitter 102
back pack 109
bedtime 105–6
benefits 117–18
bereavement, support groups 120, 124
blood tests 22
bottle feeding 39
boy, preference for 10
breastfeeding 39–42
   and conception 11–12
   and jealousy 40–1
   in pregnancy 41
   and regression 53
   support groups 42, 119, 122
buggy 108–11

Caesarean birth 36, 120
   support group 120
car seats 111–12
car travel 111–13
carrycot 110
child abuse 58
   sexual 83
   support groups 120, 122–3
childbirth 33–6
   Caesarean *see* Caesarean birth
   home or hospital 28–30
   preparing for 32–5
   presence of older child 31–2
   support groups 119, 122
child care 16, 107–8
   during hospital birth 29
   during pregnancy 21
   father's role 89–90
   support groups 122
childminder 107
   support groups 122
chorionic villus sampling *see* CVS
classes, refresher 32–3
clingy behaviour 51–2
coil (IUD) 12
comparisons (between children) 68–9
conceiving, difficulties 16–18
conflict, sibling 63, 76–81
contraception 11–13, 121
contraceptive pill 12
contraceptive sponge 13
coping, tips on 77–81
corporal punishment 71–2, 81, 121
counselling 9, 67
   addresses 120, 123
crying problems, support group 120
CVS 23–4

dangerous work 114
depression 17
  post-natal 6, 15, 58
diaphragm (cap) 12
diet 46–7, 121
difficult behaviour 51–7, 68
disability
  antenatal tests 22–4
  coping with 59–60
  and favouritism 65
  support groups 60, 120
discipline 71–2
dislike of child 66
dismissal from work 114
distress in child 27–8
divorce, support groups 121–3
doctor, attitudes of 21, 30
Domino scheme 29
double buggy 109
Down's Syndrome 15, 16, 22–3
  support groups 120

eating 46–7
education
  schools 71
  support groups 119, 121
emotions 42–3, 47
employer 19
epidural 35–6
equality of treatment 64–5
evenings 104–5
exclusion, father's 95
extended family 2

fairness 64
family 2, 19
  counsellor 9, 67
  planning 11–13, 121, 125
  position in, 73–5
  size 8
  therapy 84
father 87–99
  and birth 90–1
  jealousy 40
  and older child 28, 45, 89
  parental role 44–5, 87–8
  paternity leave 46, 91–2
  relationship with partner 94–5
  and second pregnancy 88–90
  support groups 120

favouritism 43–5, 64, 84–6
  questionnaire 84–5
  and sex of child 75–6
feeding
  breast or bottle 39–41
  tandem 41–2
  weaning 41–2
fertility 10, 17
financial considerations 16, 92–3, 108
first child 73–4
  and age gap 14–16
  difficult behaviour 51–7
  and father 28
  introduction to new baby 37–9
  jealousy 14, 40–1, 49–50
  needs 57–8
  presence at birth 31–2
  reaction to new baby 14, 38, 47–9, 56
  reaction to pregnancy 25–8
  sharing 50–1
  sleep problems 51
  weaning 41–2

gap, age 13–16
gas and air 36
gifted child, addresses 121–2
grandparents 5, 105, 107

health, mother's 15, 16
help, partner's 46
home, safety in 113
home birth 30, 38
  support group 124
hospital 37–9, 122
  births 28–30, 33
hostility to new baby 56
housework
  priorities 104
  and sexual stereotyping 75–6
hyperactivity, support group 121

illness, support groups 120–1, 123
infertility, secondary 17
intrauterine device (IUD) 12
iron 21

jealousy, father's 40
jealousy, sibling 10, 49–51, 61, 64
  and age gap 14, 50
  and breastfeeding 40–1

comparisons 68–9
difficult behaviour 51–7
and position in family 73–5
job *see* work

La Lèche League 42, 122
labelling children 69–71
labour 32, 33–6
difficult 6, 15, 32–3
laissez-faire attitude 71
large family 8–9
late baby 10
love, equal 65–6

masturbation 83
maternity
allowance 117
clothes 20
leave 15, 115–16
pay 116–17
payment, Social Fund 117–18
rights and benefits 114–18, 119, 122
menopause 10
middle child 74–5
midwife 21
miscarriage
support groups 22–3
and tests in pregnancy 22–3
mixed marriages 96–7
mixed-race child 9
money 16, 92–3, 108
morning sickness 21–2
mother
feelings about new baby 42–3
health of 15, 16
older 15, 16, 17, 22, 42
multiple births, support group 124

National Childbirth Trust 42
negative reinforcement 81
nursery 102
support groups 122

older child *see* first child
older mother 15, 16, 17, 42
antenatal tests 22
only child 6–8, 62

pain relief in labour 35–6
partnership of parents 96–7
part-time work 115
paternity leave 46, 91–92
pethidine 36
physical punishment 71–2, 81, 121
play
father's role 88
support groups 123
playgroup 102
support groups 123
playpen 113
position in family 73–5
positive reinforcement 81
post-natal depression 6, 15, 58
baby blues 45–7
support groups 58, 120, 122
posture, during pregnancy 20
practical considerations 100–13
of age gap 15
pregnancy, second 19–22
accidental 6, 10, 11–13
and breastfeeding 41
difficulties in conceiving 16–18
telling older child 25–6
tests during 22–5
premature babies, support groups 120, 123
puerperal psychosis 58
punishment 65, 71–2, 78

quarrels, sibling 63, 77–80

refresher classes 32–3
regression 52–3
rejection of mother 55
rest 20–1
rivalry, sibling 10, 61–4, 70

safety at home 113
schools 71
second child 73–4
second marriage 9
secondary infertility 17
self-esteem of child 64, 68
self-help groups *see* support groups
separation, support groups 122
Sex Discrimination Act 114
Australia 124
sex of child
and favouritism 75–6
prenatal tests 24
'right' 10–11, 42

siblings 82
sex play 82–4
sexual abuse 83
sexual relationship 97–8
sharing 50, 61–4, 78
   rooms 106
sheath 12
shopping 110–11
   support groups 124
siblings
   closeness of 7–8, 63
   rivalry 10, 61–4, 70
   schools 71
   sex of 82
   sex play 82–4
sickness in pregnancy 21–2
single parent 8
   support groups 121–2
sleep problems 50
   support groups 120
sling 108
smacking 71–2, 81
Social Fund Maternity Payment 117–18
space 106–7
spina bifida 22
Statutory Maternity Pay (SMP) 116–17
stepfamilies 84, 96
   support groups 84, 124
stereotyping of children 69–71
   sexual roles 75–6
stress 77–81
   support groups 123–4
Supermum 103–4

support
   groups 42, 58, 60, 84, 119–25
   networks 90

tandem buggy 111
tandem feeding 41–2
tests in pregnancy 22–5
third child 8–9, 11
time 100–3
   father's 93
   together 95–6, 103
   with baby 102
   with older child 101
tiredness 20
transport 109–13

ultrasound scan 22

value judgements 68–70

weaning 41–2
withdrawal 51–2
work, father's 93–4
work, mother's 21, 104–5
   and age gap 15, 16
   child care 107
   dangerous 114
   delaying return 115–16
   dismissal 114
   maternity leave 115–16
   rights 114–18, 124–5
   support groups 124

youngest child 75

Also available from Unwin Paperbacks and Pandora Press

BOOK OF CHILD CARE
Dr Hugh Jolly

This new, fully revised, updated and illustrated paperback edition of Dr Hugh Jolly's *Book of Child Care* remains the most comprehensive guide of its kind. It conveys in detail everything about children that new and experienced parents need reference to, from the newborn through the early months to school age and beyond. All facets of daily child care are included and any topic can be found through the extensively cross referenced index. New developments are all covered here, and Dr Jolly answers questions regularly asked by parents and others with skill, wisdom, commonsense and humour. Advice is also given for the management of both mild and serious childhood illnesses.

NEW ACTIVE BIRTH
Janet Balaskas

New Active Birth will help you and your partner to prepare for and experience an Active Birth. Throughout time and the world over, women have chosen to actively find the most comfortable positions for labour and birth. It is only we in the West who have the extraordinary notion that a woman should lie on her back in a position of helplessness that defies the laws of nature and gravity.

With this book by Janet Balaskas, founder of the Active Birth Movement, you can learn to develop all your body's resources to deal with the instinctive experience of childbirth. It is also for partners, teachers, midwives and everyone involved, to help mothers get up off the delivery table and to bring back some of the commonsense which has been overlooked by modern obstetrics.

HOW TO HAVE A BABY AND STAY SANE
Virginia Ironside

How to Have a Baby and Stay Sane tackles the tricky areas of pregnancy, birth, hospital, feeding, travelling, working and generally coping. It's an outrageously funny, sensitive and ultimately caring and loving book for mothers who are determined to do right by their babies, and desperately guilty and anxious that they are getting it wrong.

This entertaining, commonsense book is illustrated with sharp and witty cartoons, and is the perfect gift for all aspiring and present mums and dads.

CHILDREN'S FOOD: THE GOOD, THE BAD AND THE USELESS
Dr Tim Lobstein

In *Children's Food: The Good, the Bad and the Useless*, Dr Tim Lobstein, specialist in children's food and nutrition at the London Food Commission, unravels the mysteries. He shows whose interests official regulations are really protecting. He demonstrates how far the interests of the manufacturers and distributors outweigh those of the consumer. He highlights particular risks and dangers that we run when we buy food for our children and he decodes the mysteries of food labels.

Dr Lobstein ends on a practical note by describing what a properly balanced diet should contain, and he lists the types of food that really are good for children.

THE A–Z OF FEEDING IN THE FIRST YEAR
Heather Welford

This highly informative book sets out to answer all the questions that arise during the crucial first year. Over 300 entries covers topics from A to Z explaining, defining and describing every aspect of feeding a baby and the changeover from milk-only to family meals. *The A–Z of Feeding in the First Year* includes helpful illustrations and a clearly laid out recipe section for simple, nutritious and tasty dishes for baby and the rest of the family as well.

Heather Welford writes for every new parent, offering sound information and sensible advice, with sympathy and humour.

THE ILLUSTRATED DICTIONARY OF PREGNANCY AND BIRTH
Heather Welford

The Illustrated Dictionary of Pregnancy and Birth has over 450 entries – from Alphafetoprotein to Old Wives' Tales; Apgar Test to Maternity Leave; Braxton-Hicks Contractions to Zygote; Dental Checks to Vernix – and many clear and helpful illustrations. Comprehensive and straightforward, it includes everything you'll need to know for a happy, healthy pregnancy and birth.

Heather Welford has called on her own experience and research, and the advice of a leading obstetrician and a midwife to compile all the information both a new or experienced mother could want, in an attractive and accessible format.

BIRTH AND OUR BODIES
Paddy O'Brien

Working chronologically from pre-conception right through to the birth itself, this guide provides a comprehensive exercise programme for relaxation, combating morning sickness and stage fright in the last few weeks of pregnancy, and for strengthening the pelvic floor muscles.

Illustrated with line drawings from 'life', *Birth and Our Bodies* helps mothers to stay in touch with their own bodies, and in charge of them, when they seem in danger of being taken over by the baby. So, as well as maintaining and strengthening your muscles you will get stronger and more supple emotionally.

UNTIL THEY ARE FIVE
Angela Phillips

Until They are Five covers every aspect of child care, from small babies to five year olds. It will help you make vital decisions about your child's welfare, enjoy her development to the full, and cope with daily disasters – or a real crisis. Unlike other child care books, this one will not make you feel guilty or inadequate. There is always more than one way of bringing up a child. Be it weaning, toilet training or learning to walk, one child will behave differently from another. Angela Phillips discusses alternative approaches, and leaves you free to explore what is best for you and your child.

Comprehensive and comforting, this is a parent-to-parent guide, based on women's real experiences.

YOUR BODY, YOUR BABY, YOUR LIFE
Angela Phillips, with Nicky Leap and Barbara Jacobs

Your Body, Your Baby, Your Life starts with help on planning for pregnancy six months before you conceive, stays with you up to and through the birth and sees you safely into the world of new parenthood. It equips you with the information you need to work with health professionals, giving you a voice in your own care and allowing you to make decisions about the pregnancy and labour that you want.

It includes information on choices in antenatal treatment and the place of birth, preparing yourself mentally and physically for childbirth, recognising problems and assessing the help you are offered, tests and their side effects, understanding your rights and claiming benefits, your body after pregnancy, living with a new baby, returning to work, and much more.

0 04 649045 4	BOOK OF CHILD CARE Dr Hugh Jolly	£8.99 ☐
0 04 440388 7	NEW ACTIVE BIRTH Janet Balaskas	£7.99 ☐
0 04 440316 X	HOW TO HAVE A BABY AND STAY SANE Virginia Ironside	£5.99 ☐
0 04 440251 1	THE A–Z OF FEEDING IN THE FIRST YEAR Heather Welford	£3.95 ☐
0 04 612047 5	THE ILLUSTRATED DICTIONARY OF PREGNANCY AND BIRTH Heather Welford	£3.95 ☐
0 04 440300 3	CHILDREN'S FOOD: THE GOOD, THE BAD AND THE USELESS Dr Tim Lobstein	£3.95 ☐
0 86358 047 5	BIRTH AND OUR BODIES Paddy O'Brien	£4.50 ☐
0 04 440361 5	UNTIL THEY ARE FIVE Angela Phillips	£4.99 ☐
0 86358 006 8	YOUR BODY, YOUR BABY, YOUR LIFE Angela Phillips, Nicky Leap and Barbara Jacobs	£4.95 ☐

All these books are available at your local bookshop or newsagent, or can be ordered direct by post. Just tick the titles you want and fill in the form below.

Name ....

Address ....

....

....

Write to Unwin Cash Sales, PO Box 11, Falmouth, Cornwall TR10 9EN.

Please enclose remittance to the value of the cover price plus:

UK: 80p for the first book plus 20p for each additional book ordered to a maximum charge of £2.00

BFPO: 80p for the first book and 20p for each additional book

OVERSEAS INC EIRE: £1.50 for the first book plus £1.00 for the second book and 30p for each additional book

Unwin Paperbacks reserve the right to show new retail prices on the covers, which may differ from those previously advertised in the text or elsewhere. Postage rates are also subject to revision.